The
BLT
Cookbook

Also by Michele Anna Jordan

Our Favorite Sandwich

The BLT Cookbook

Michele Anna Jordan

WILLIAM MORROW
An Imprint of HarperCollins*Publishers*

HarperCollins books may be purchased for educational, business, or sales promotional use. For information please write: Special Markets Department, HarperCollins Publishers Inc., 10 East 53rd Street, New York, NY 10022.

FIRST EDITION

Designed by William Ruoto

"Toothpick" art by Daria Amato Greiner

Printed on acid-free paper

Library of Congress Cataloging-in-Publication Data

Jordan, Michele Anna.
    The BLT cookbook : Our Favorite Sandwich/ Michele Anna Jordan.—1st ed.
        p.   cm.
    Includes index.
    ISBN 0-06-008773-0
    1. Cookery (Pork)   2. Bacon.   3. Lettuce.   4. Cookery (Tomatoes)   I. Title.

TX749.5.P67 J67 2003
641.8'4—dc21

2002068847

03 04 05 06 07 WBC/QW 10 9 8 7 6 5 4 3 2

for Gina and Nicolle
and for Lucas

Contents

Acknowledgments

I extend a big rasher of thanks to everyone whose eyes lit up when I mentioned this project, some of whom I know by name, some of whom I met only in passing, at a wine tasting, a cooking class, a farmers' market. This book belongs to all of you, because without that twinkle in your eyes I may not have written it, so worried was I that my fascination with the BLT was a solo passion. Thanks for assuring me otherwise.

Special thanks to Harriet Bell for appreciating the spirit of the book, and rising to its occasion not once, but twice. And to my agent, Amy Rennert, for moving things along quickly. And to Frances Bowles, copyeditor with both heart and soul, thank you again, for everything.

Thank you, too, to Dennis Pocekay, a doctor in Petaluma, California, and an enthusiastic cook and culinary student, for the on-line research. And to Bill Niman, for his work with family pig farmers in Iowa and for making great bacon so much more accessible than it has been in recent years. And to Susan Goss of Zinfandel Restaurant in Chicago, I raise a glass of Pinot Noir in gratitude for your wonderful recipe and the speed with which you provided it. To Lou Preston, thank you for the always sensational bread, which flatters any BLT. And to Mark Braunstein, thanks for the tip about chowhound.com (which came years before the article in *The New Yorker*).

Without all of the backyard gardeners who care so tenderly for their heirloom tomatoes, our BLTs would be a shadow of what they are with their fruit. Thank you and keep it up!

I'd also like to acknowledge the fishermen of Bodega Bay, especially Jan Butler, who despite astonishing odds continued to fish for wild king salmon until his tragic death on July 16, 2002.

Thanks once again to John Kramer, Nancy Dobbs, Andrew Dobbs-Kramer, James Carroll, John Boland, Jeanine Richardson, and Betty Ellsworth for the love, friendship, and support that keeps me going.

To Gina and Nicolle, my sweet girls, thank you thank you thank you. And to little Lucas, born as we were negotiating the sale of this book: it won't be long before you, too, will savor the pleasures of the simple little sandwich that nourished both your mama and me.

Introduction

"Wonder Bread slathered with Hellman's mayonnaise," I read one dusky winter morning, "goes a long way toward making you just stupidly happy for three or four hours."

I was perusing chowhound.com, a website devoted to conversational postings by enthusiastic eaters (not foodies!) the world around, looking for partners in passion. Posting after posting confirmed my long-standing suspicion that I am not alone in my profound affection for the BLT. I found tips for BLTs in Rhode Island, Maryland, Virginia, California, and all over Manhattan.

I didn't agree with everything I read. "Miracle Whip?" I shouted at my tangerine iMac. "Oscar Meyer bacon?" I asked out loud, shaking my head. "Replace the lettuce with melted Stilton? Now there's an interesting twist." I smiled. Soon I was laughing. Chowhound is like that: its sheer exuberance is irresistible.

I had lost my mad race to finish this book before tomato season ended. Until the first frost, I had been in the full lather of creativity, a rainbow of colorful tomatoes from local farmers lining my kitchen counters. I savored BLTs in their myriad variations and experimented with pastas, salads, and soups inspired by that holy trinity of tastes: acid, salt, and smoky, voluptuous pork fat. I made sandwich after sandwich, each with a different variety of tomato. At a farmers' market in Healdsburg, I discovered one, the Black Brandywine, a burgundy-colored beefsteak tomato, that became my favorite of the season. I taped a screen test for a television show using a recipe developed for this book.

But by the time I was ready to begin writing, winter had set in and tomatoes were just a memory. That's when I found Chowhound. The exuberance of the postings, the site's utter lack of pretension, and the various trails I followed—including ones that led me to a website devoted to mayonnaise and one called the Condiment Packet Museum—revived my flagging winter spirits. Summer began to seem inevitable, and the book once again made sense to me. Gloom transformed into longing and anticipation. One morning I fried up some of my homemade bacon, saved the drippings for risotto, and shared a couple of rashers with Poe, my long-haired black cat, who sits beside me now as I write. After he nibbled the last little piece, he licked the drippings from my fingers then moved to my chin and my lips. Ah, bacon; it is irresistible. I started my tomatoes early and pampered them with special mulch.

BLT began as a labor of love. I wanted to write about BLTs because I love them and believe there are a multitude of others who feel as I do. A BLT is a lighthearted pleasure, like a fragment of a favorite song heard unexpectedly as you walk along the street, or a commercial for an Apple computer that leaves you sitting on the couch with a silly smile on your face. A good BLT soothes both minor annoyances and major problems, at least briefly.

Among a BLT's myriad powers is an ability to cure nausea, especially morning sickness. During my first pregnancy, simple craving led me to salvation, which I found in a classic little diner next to the office where I worked after school. I sat on a red vinyl stool shabby with age, at a long beige Formica counter and ate a BLT. I can see it now as I write, the Wonder Bread toasted golden brown, the smear of Best Foods mayonnaise, the thin rounds of pale red tomatoes, the cool emerald glow of iceberg lettuce, and those two strips of edible salvation, the bacon. I returned to my desk light and happy, my nausea quelled. When it returned, so did my craving for another BLT.

With my daughter not quite a year old, I suddenly found myself longing for my favorite sandwich. Uh oh. My craving grew to enormous proportions. I ate BLTs for breakfast, for lunch, for dinner. I wanted nothing else. Gina's sister Nicolle was born eight months later.

Sometimes I look at my two beautiful daughters and think to myself: flesh of my flesh, blood of my blood, you are made of bacon, lettuce, and tomato. Flesh of my flesh, I think, just look at what the BLT has made.

A BLT is reliable, too, a security blanket on a plate: even the worst one isn't all that bad. Sometimes, in the middle of summer when you've harvested your first tomato or in early fall, when the light changes to a golden glow that breaks your heart with its fragile beauty, or some late night at a truck stop on the Interstate, a BLT is enough. In times of trouble, that's a good thing to remember. When all else fails, try a BLT.

In Praise of the BLT

First, there's the smoky aroma of bacon, and the sound of it sizzling. You're salivating already, aren't you? Next comes the warm, yeasty smell of bread as you slice it, and the evocative scent as it toasts. The tomato is plump, smooth, and heavy in your hand, the lettuce cool and refreshing. It's hard to resist plunging a finger into that luscious mayonnaise, so go ahead: a fingerful, licked off slowly as the bread turns color.

The Bacon-Lettuce-and-Tomato sandwich is one of America's finest inventions, far better than the ubiquitous hamburger for which we are known the world around. Don't get me wrong: there are great hamburgers, but they are not to be found in the fast-food joints that deface the globe like old grease spots on your favorite tee shirt. From an upscale bistro in San Francisco and a shabby diner in Manhattan to an old inn in Fairbanks, Alaska, you'll find succulent burgers of hand-ground, hand-formed beef with character and flavor and style, made by someone for the simple love of it. But these are not the burgers for which America is known, and I hang my head when I consider what most of the world thinks of as American cuisine. I wish I could make everyone a BLT. That would be the end of the golden arches, I'm sure of it.

There are times when the BLT just tastes *right,* primal and true, the best thing you could ever eat. The play of salt and acid, the silk of the tomato against the salt crunch of the bacon, the crisp refreshing pulse of lettuce, the juicy mingling of mayonnaise and tomato drippings: it is sheer delight. And if you need your pleasures imbued with sin, if guilt heightens your delight, this is a sandwich for you. The nutritionists wag their fingers: "Mayonnaise is bad for you! You should not eat bacon!" When it comes to guilty pleasures, it's hard to beat a BLT.

If you eat to live, you may never have had a moment transformed by a nibble or a bite, or felt the world and its worries recede as you savor the smoke, the salt, the fat, the sweet silky sass. If you've read this far, you are probably certain that I'm a bit loony. But if you live to eat, you know exactly what I'm saying. By the middle of winter, you are dreaming of summer's tomatoes, anticipating the scent of the bacon, and plotting your strategy. Perhaps you should order a loaf of Poilâne's famous bread from Paris. Better yet, maybe you should get going on that outdoor brick oven so you can bake your own. Will the Northern Lights ripen before the Black Brandywines? Will you have the discipline to wait, or will you cave with the first Early Girls? Then you make yourself a Bloody Mary, stoke the fire, and sigh. Summer seems so far away when you have a BLT jones.

So what makes a great BLT? The ones you find in mediocre diners, the ones with mealy tomatoes, microwaved bacon, airy bread, and iceberg lettuce surely don't warrant all this excitement, yet mention a BLT and about half the population gets all squirmy and misty eyed.

It's really very simple to make a sensational BLT; there's no secret and no single formula for success. Just give it great ingredients, and the sandwich will do the rest. I offer my best advice and favorite finds in these pages, and encourage you to experiment. But if you've been limiting your hunting grounds to the supermarket, it's time to brave new terrain: get thee to the farmers' market, the corner butcher shop, that cool new bakery.

Stalking the Perfect Tomato

> Homegrown tomatoes, homegrown tomatoes,
> What'd life be without homegrown tomatoes?
> Only two things that money can't buy,
> And that's true love and homegrown tomatoes.
> —Guy Clark, "Homegrown Tomatoes"

The bacon, the bread, the lettuce, the mayonnaise: there are no insurmountable hurdles to prevent you from getting the best of each of these. Maybe you have to drive across town for bread, or ask a friend in Berkeley to FedEx a loaf of Acme, but good bread *can* be had. There's plenty of great bacon, if not at your neighborhood market, then at the nearest gourmet shop or by mail. East of the Rockies, there's Hellman's mayonnaise; west, it's called Best Foods but it's the same thing. Lettuce is never a problem.

But that damn tomato. It refuses to submit to human whim or desire. Withholding itself until late June or July or even mid-August, depending on where you live, it keeps the BLT a seasonal creature. Hothouse tomatoes, tomatoes from the Southern Hemisphere, out-of-season tomatoes from Florida or Mexico: they just don't cut it. Commercial tomatoes are har-

Heirloom Tomato Festival

There are many tomato festivals in the United States, but for dedicated tomato lovers with a healthy sense of adventure, the most interesting may be Kendall-Jackson Winery's Heirloom Tomato Festival, held in early September in Santa Rosa, the heart of Sonoma County wine country. There are many attractions—tomatoes prepared every which way, a tomato art show, music, wine—but what interests us is the tasting of heirlooms, 118 varieties at last count, all from the winery's extensive gardens. For tickets, visit www.kj.com/events/tomato.

vested before they ripen, ethylene gas makes them turn red, and thick skins help them survive the long trip to your local market. These poor tomatoes spend countless hours in refrigerated trucks, their flesh growing mealy in the cool temperatures. If you want a great BLT, you have to wait until tomatoes ripen near you.

And what about all those heirloom varieties, the knobbly marbled spheres, the green-ripe globes, the pink, the near white, the blood red? No longer is it a simple matter to choose tomatoes by holding them in your palm, one at a time, and judging their relative heft—a good, juicy tomato will be heavy for its size—or by gently pressing their flesh in search of just the right amount of give. Now you must choose among a rainbow of colors, a panorama of sizes, an encyclopedia of names. If you select the wrong variety, will that perfect BLT remain elusive?

Of course not. There is no single variety that will transform a mundane BLT into perfection on toast, regardless of what people from New Jersey tell you. The vast selection is merely an opportunity for indulgence. What matters most is that a tomato is grown naturally without a bunch of chemical pesticides and fertilizers, allowed to ripen on the vine, and kept at room temperature until it is devoured.

Actual genetic differences between varieties, no matter how visually dramatic, are minuscule; a tomato is as nearly influenced by soil and climate as by genes. Heirloom varieties can be marvelous, with gorgeous colors and shapes and subtle variations in flavor: sweet, tart, spicy, fragrant, salty. But common hybrids, grown with care, can be as delicious as even the most pampered antique tomato.

The Alchemy of Bacon

You can make a good tomato sandwich, even a great tomato sandwich, without bacon. A tomato sandwich is a wonderful thing; but add bacon and that sandwich leaps heavenward. It

Tomato Bliss

My own idea of pure bliss is the tomato sandwich, which is good on any kind of bread, from grainy imported *volkornbrot* to suave, textureless semolina. This sandwich can only be made with ripe tomatoes, luscious and full of seeds. The bread is slathered with mayonnaise, then dusted with celery salt and layered with thinly sliced tomatoes. I prefer this sandwich open, but it is fine with a lid.

—Laurie Colwin, *More Home Cooking*

becomes sublime, more than the sum of its parts, more than simply better than the same sandwich without the bacon. Bacon is the sorcerer's stone; its subtle alchemy transforms the base sandwich into gold.

American bacon, that fatty rasher with stripes of lean meat running through it, is made from the bellies of pigs. You can cure other cuts, but they won't be the same. You'll end with something *lean*. For a BLT, you want smoky salty pork fat. Now and then, pancetta—unsmoked cured pork belly from Italy—is good on a BLT. But as a steady diet, even it leaves you craving something more.

Bacon is a simple thing. After a pork belly is trimmed, it is rubbed with salt and left to cure until the salt penetrates the meat. Then the meat is exposed to smoke but not heat for anywhere from a few hours to several days.

Alas, very little bacon is made this way. Most bacon is injected with brine, smoke flavorings, and various other ingredients—just read the back of any package. By weight, commercial bacon is in large part water. If you notice shrinkage as you cook it, that is because the water evaporates in the pan. The water also makes the bacon curl, and pop, and spit. Some premium bacon is cured in brine rather than dry, a technique that is better than injecting the brine but not as good as the dry-cure method.

There's another problem. Corporate farmers have taken the pig far from its natural environment and, in a response to America's recent fear of fat, have also created leaner pigs. Of course, this lean pork is not as flavorful as pork raised the old-fashioned way; pigs are by nature fat and that fat keeps the meat moist and tender. Of even greater concern are the wretched lives that these pigs live and the serious environmental damage caused by their prodigious quantities of waste.

Happy Hogs

Although Bill Niman made a name for himself with beef, the first meat animals he raised were pigs, back in the early 1970s. He has gone on to produce some of the country's finest natural beef, for years available only at high-end restaurants. In the 1990s, Niman expanded into retail markets, offering not just premium beef but also lamb and outrageously delicious pork.

Bringing Home the Bacon

He wore a hat
And he had a job
And he brought home the bacon
So that no one knew.
—Devo, "Mongoloid"

The origin of "bringing home the bacon," which today means being the primary source of family income, may be lost to history, but there is plenty of interesting speculation. Two stories can be traced back to twelfth-century England, where it was the custom for local churches to give young couples a slab of bacon if they were still happy a year after the wedding. In the small town of Dunmow, the local pastor is said to have offered a side of bacon to any married man willing to swear in front of the congregation that he had not quarreled with his wife for a year and a day. Bringing home the bacon became a source of pride and respect.

Niman Ranch works with small family farmers in Iowa. The pigs are fed neither hormones nor antibiotics, they live outdoors with access to the mud puddles in which they cool themselves (pigs don't have sweat glands), and to the hay-lined birthing huts the sows prefer. You can buy Niman bacon through the website (www.nimanranch.com); a full list of retail outlets is included on the site.

R. M. Felts Packing Co. in Virginia has been curing ham and bacon since the 1930s. The extraordinary bacon, which fries up perfectly crisp and pale golden brown, explodes in your mouth like tiny star bursts of succulent smoky fat. Felts bacon is cured in salt for two weeks, cold smoked for three days, dried in a warm room for a week, and rubbed with crushed black peppercorns. It is sold on or off the bone (the bones are great simmered with beans, collard greens, or potatoes), sliced or unsliced. If you want it unsmoked, you can get it that way, too. Felts ships the bacon all over the world. The company does not have a web site; reach it at (757) 859-6131.

To Toast or Not to Toast?

The imprint bread makes upon our memories is strange and compelling. We never crave the lousy tomatoes of our youth, and I've yet to meet anyone with a nostalgic fondness for bad bacon. Yet the bread we eat as children has a visceral hold on us, regardless of its quality. If mama served us Wonder Bread, Wonder Bread satisfies an emotional longing nothing else can touch.

In the past two decades, there has been a transformation in the bread available in the United States. Some experts feel that our best surpass the breads of Europe and, because I live

The Bacon-a-Month Club

"Bacon is like sex in a skillet."

—Dan Phillips, founder

Dan Phillips is to bacon what Barry Levenson, the founder of the Mount Horeb Mustard Museum, is to mustard, a dedicated devotee, with an abundance of passion, silliness, and entrepreneurial spirit. Levenson sells "Poupon U" sweatshirts and has a running schtick protesting mayonnaise and ketchup. His museum caught the attention of David Letterman, who invited Levenson to dinner.

Phillips's website, gratefulpalate.com, offers bacon-shaped soap and tasting notes that rival those of *Wine X* magazine. Consider the description of Summerfield Farm Bacon: "A great big hedonistic pig bomb. Like bacon pudding. Rich, super intense flavors. The Château d'Yquem of pig." His club has been featured in Jay Leno's monologue on *The Tonight Show*.

Phillips offers what may be the largest collection— nearly three dozen at last count—of artisan bacons available at a single location. Bacon junkies can sign up for one or two pounds a month.

in northern California, the heart of the country's bread revolution, I concur. Acme Bakery in Berkeley started it all in the early 1980s. Acme's sour bâtard and *pain levain* make excellent BLTs; when you're making a club, its white bread can't be beat.

My favorite bread for BLTs will not be yours unless you

live near me. Look for breads made close to home by artisan bakers and experiment until you find one that tastes just right. I prefer Italian hearth-style loaves, made with mostly white flour and a sour starter. Bread with big air holes is my favorite, in spite of its inconvenience: mayonnaise drips out of the holes and sometimes other ingredients fall out, too. But I transform the mess into a treat; after enjoying the sandwich, which I eat over a plate, I roll my finger in the mayonnaise, scrumptious with the juices of bacon and tomato, and lick it off. Yum!

When in an earlier book, *The Good Cook's Book of Tomatoes* (1995), I suggested that toasting is optional, a critic took me to task for even hinting that the bread might go untoasted. "Is she crazy?" is how I think she put it. Duly chastised, I have never again offered the suggestion, but the first BLT I ever ate was on untoasted bread and so it has a special place in my taste memory. When making the first BLT of the year, sometimes I toast the bread and sometimes I don't, especially when the bread is absolutely fresh.

As a general rule, bread should be toasted. The aroma of toast is the ideal foreplay; it makes us begin to salivate, much as the smell of frying bacon does. The texture of toasted bread helps the sandwich maintain its structure, too, rather than become soggy. The degree is crucial, though. I recommend letting the bread turn a light golden brown over about a third of its surface. If toasted more, it becomes hard and brittle, and its dark taste trumps the other ingredients.

The Green Thing

The key to the green part of a BLT is freshness. Few things are worse than old, limp lettuce. If you have a garden, it's simple to walk outside and snip a few leaves while the bacon's frying. If not, you'll find the best lettuce at farmers' markets.

Several types of lettuce flatter BLTs. The first three layers of a head of iceberg offer the classic taste and texture of a traditional BLT, but the leaves must be absolutely crisp. Further in on the head, the texture and taste are wrong; these inner leaves should not be used on a BLT. The reverse is the case with butter lettuce; the inner leaves have a more delicate texture and subtle flavor than do the outer leaves, which can be tough.

Sandwiches with crunchy additions such as soft-shell crab or crisp leeks are best with soft, tender lettuces. With smooth additions—avocado, say, or smoked mozzarella—add extra crunch with iceberg or romaine. But always put freshness first, and use the best lettuce you have, regardless of variety.

Other greens can be good on a BLT. Arugula is excellent, though it is best in cold weather. If you love it, grow your own in a cool, shady spot, give it lots of water, and pinch off flowers as they form. Watercress adds a peppery crunch that is both refreshing and delicious. Bitter chicories such as frisée and radicchio are not right for BLTs, nor are spinach, dandelion greens, mustard

The Problem

A BLT is my favorite sandwich and they're so hard to find. In most cases the bacon is done ahead or isn't crisp enough, the tomatoes aren't ripe, the mayo isn't slathered on with abandon, and they try to upgrade the sandwich with other greens rather than crisp, cold iceberg.

—Michael Bauer, restaurant critic and food editor, *San Francisco Chronicle*

greens, or kales; the strong flavors and substantial textures interfere with the alchemy of ingredients.

Be sure to put any greens on top of the bacon, not under the tomato, where they will act as an unwanted shield between the tomato and the mayonnaise, which need to be flush up against each other for proper mingling.

Never Hold the Mayo

Mayonnaise is as essential as the other ingredients are—the unifying element that adds a voluptuousness that cannot be duplicated by olive oil, cheese, or anything else found in nature or invented by man. Mayonnaise is a must on a BLT, and there has to be enough of it, not just a stingy smear that disappears into the bread. Life is short. Live! Indulge! *Slather!* And when it comes to brands, you have just two choices: Best Foods west of the

Rockies; Hellman's east of the Rockies. Sometimes life is refreshingly simple.

The so-called healthier versions of this classic French egg-and-oil sauce are not worth exploring; their lack of lusciousness and their inferior flavors leave you restless, pensive, and unsatisfied. Besides, the BLT is a seasonal creature, not something you eat daily year-round. And, darlin', with all that bacon, do you really think low-fat mayonnaise is going to make much difference?

There is one acceptable alternative: homemade mayonnaise. Sometimes it is the best choice, especially when you make a garlicky aïoli, a delightful flourish after you've had your fill of the traditional sandwich, or when you want the pure smooth sensuousness that only handmade mayonnaise offers.

I must add a few words about that imposter, Miracle Whip. Its cloying sweetness makes a BLT taste flabby and, without the spark of lemon provided by mayonnaise, the sandwich loses its zip. I am aware that Miracle Whip has its fans and that many of them do slather it onto BLTs. It's an East Coast thing, some tell me. You're not southern, you wouldn't understand, others say. It may have that same nostalgic, physical resonance that Wonder Bread does, but still, I can't even think about it. If it's your preference, please don't tell me.

Bacchus and the BLT

Iced tea in a Mason jar, hand-squeezed lemonade, a cold beer, a Coke: these are the most popular drinks with a BLT. But what if you want to dress things up, serve a nice wine, try something different? With a little thought, the perfect match is a cinch.

Red wine with meat, Burgundy with bacon: if you need

rules, this one isn't bad. The smoke and fat of bacon call out for a red and the salt requires a good bit of acid, hence Burgundy, the geographic term for Pinot Noir.

Pinot Noir flatters a BLT, which in turn flatters the wine. The delicate toastiness of the bread, the sweet acidity of the tomato, the tangy lusciousness of the mayonnaise, all of these elements resonate with a well-made Pinot Noir, which is to say, one

The World's Biggest BLT

Imagine a BLT that stretches for dozens of feet, covering table after table nearly as far as you can see. In September 2003, I will construct such as sandwich, the World's Biggest BLT, at the Kendall-Jackson Winery Heirloom Tomato Festival. Assisting me will be students from WOW!, the Worth our Weight Culinary School for delinquent teens founded by the chef Evelyn Cheatham. We'll use propane torches to toast the bread, made by Craig Ponsford of Artisan Bakers. Tomatoes will be from the winery's garden, just a few feet from the sandwich. The bacon will be dry-cured from Niman Ranch and the mayonnaise, of course, will be Best Foods. Jennifer Sheehan and Anne Hayes, who operate Sisters Farm in Sebastopol, will plant a row of lettuce for the sandwich project. After the BLT is assembled and its length certified by representatives of the Guinness Book of World Records, we'll sell it for $2.00 an inch and donate the money to the school. Patrick McGuinn, a friend and filmmaker (*SPF 2000, Kill Me Tomorrow, Baby Blue*) from Los Angeles, is producing a short documentary about the sandwich.

that is made in the vineyard. Left to itself, Pinot Noir is delicate yet complex, with elements of strawberry, cherry, raspberry, mushrooms, smoke, tobacco, leather, and yes, sometimes even bacon. Its tannins are smooth and silky.

Beaujolais, Côtes-du-Rhône, and Rhône-style reds from California are excellent with our little sandwich, though Syrahs from the New World and Australia tend to sit on it. If there's one at hand, enjoy an Italian Dolcetto or Nebbiolo, both of which are perfect with a lusty BLT. The right Zinfandel can be a magical match; look for one from Dry Creek Valley that is not too high in alcohol. When the temperatures soar and you're breaking off leaves of iceberg lettuce for your sandwich, an ice-cold dry rosé—*not* a white Zinfandel, which is too sweet—is your best bet.

The sexiest companion to a BLT may be Laphroaig, a single-malt scotch from Islay, an island in the Inner Hebrides. Laphroaig is made by soaking barley in the island's root beer–colored water, which is naturally filtered through the peat that covers the island. The barley is smoked with burning peat before it is fermented. The resulting scotch has hints of salt, smoke, seaweed, leather, tobacco, and fat, not unlike bacon in a glass.

About the Recipes

These recipes are inspired by the BLT, by its seductive harmony of flavors and textures. Most were developed in my own kitchen in the simple course of my eating and cooking life. There's nothing like a platter of ripe tomatoes and some bacon in the fridge to spark creativity.

I tested all of these recipes using home equipment: a modest gas range, a stove-top grill, a backyard charcoal barbecue, and a smoker. I do, however, use a sturdy professional Cuisinart that can withstand plenty of abuse.

For salt, I use soft-flaked Diamond Crystal Kosher. My peppercorns are from Sarawak, Malaysia, and are ground in a wooden Peugeot grinder. My default bacon is Niman Ranch.

Results in your kitchen will vary and that is to be expected. Be flexible and more concerned with the goodness of a dish than with precision. Recipes such as these have a wide margin of error. As long as you use high-quality ingredients, you will be pleased with the results.

How to Cook Bacon

When I need a few slices, I fry bacon in an ordinary heavy pan, either Magnalite, All-Clad, or cast iron. Sometimes I use a Magnalite stove-top griddle, though pouring off the fat can be awkward. Any pan should have a heavy bottom that conducts heat evenly, without hot spots that burn the bacon. I preheat the pan over a medium-high flame for about 90 seconds before adding the bacon. After the bacon has released a quantity of fat, I use tongs to turn it, cook until it is golden brown, and then transfer it onto a brown paper bag to drain.

If your bacon sticks, curls, or spits, try this: bring the bacon to room temperature and arrange a single row of rashers in a cold skillet set over medium-low heat. Cook the bacon slowly and turn it frequently. To avoid its curling and spitting entirely, buy dry-cured bacon.

In nonstick pans, fat pools, much of it is reabsorbed by the bacon, and the bacon never becomes properly crisp. I never ever use a microwave; the texture is wrong in bacon cooked this way.

When feeding a large group, I cook bacon on a rimmed baking sheet in a 450°F oven. It takes about 8 minutes for thin rashers, 10 to 12 minutes for thick ones, times that vary depending on how you will use the bacon.

For crumbled bacon, you'll get better results when you cook the rasher whole and then mince it with a sharp knife. This is messier than dicing the bacon first, but the edges of raw bacon get a little hard as they cook.

Appetizer BLTs

Cocktail BLTs

The secret to a good cocktail BLT is size and shape. It must be easy to pick up with one hand and to eat in a single bite or two.

6 to 8 slices bacon

8 to 12 small tomatoes, each about 2 inches in
 diameter

36 slices good white sandwich bread

1 cup homemade Mayonnaise, with herbs or olives
 (page 125)

Kosher salt

Black pepper in a mill

½ head iceberg lettuce, outer leaves only, shredded
 (page 124)

Fry the bacon until crisp, drain on a brown paper bag, and crumble. Remove the stem core of each tomato. Cut the tomatoes into equal slices, each about ⅜ inch thick. Set aside any slices that are significantly larger or smaller than the others; you want 36 slices that are nearly identical in shape and size.

Preheat the oven to 275°F. Using a tomato slice as a guide, select a cookie or pastry cutter or a small glass of the same size. Cut

two circles of bread from each piece of bread and set them on baking sheets. Toast in the oven, turning once, until the bread is evenly browned, about 12 minutes.

Set the toasted bread on a work surface and smear a little mayonnaise on each piece. Set a tomato slice on top of each of 36 pieces of toast, season lightly with salt and pepper, and scatter a little bacon on top. Add a little lettuce, top with a remaining piece of bread, mayonnaise side down, and press gently. Arrange the sandwiches on platters and serve immediately.

Grilled BLT Kabobs

I celebrated my friend Andrew's tenth birthday with a BLT party. First on the menu were these kabobs, followed by Bruschetta (page 34) and Pappardelle with Zucchini, Bacon, and Tomato Concassé (page 132). Andrew was a willing and enthusiastic assistant in the kitchen, and no one complained that the we had bacon and tomato in every dish.

Thirty 1½-inch squares of sourdough bread
¼ cup extra virgin olive oil
Kosher salt
Black pepper in a mill
10 slices lean bacon
Ten 12-inch-long wooden skewers, soaked in water
  for 1 hour
30 cherry tomatoes
1 quart salad greens
⅓ cup handmade Aïoli (page 128), thinned with a
  little warm water or lemon juice, in a squeeze
  bottle

Prepare a fire in a charcoal grill or heat a stove-top grill.

Put the sourdough bread into a medium bowl, drizzle the olive oil over it, and toss until the bread has absorbed all the oil. Season with salt and pepper and toss again.

Fry the bacon until it is not quite crisp.

To make the kabobs, put a skewer through a slice of bacon, spearing it through the lean part near one end. Push it down about 1½ inches from the tip of the skewer. Add a bread cube, and then pierce the bacon again, so that it is folded over the bread. Add a cherry tomato and fold the bacon over that. Continue until you have 3 cubes of bread and 3 cherry tomatoes, each separated by a fold of the bacon, on each skewer.

Grill over a charcoal fire or on a stove-top grill, turning to grill the bread on each side. Toss the salad greens with a little salt and spread them over a large serving platter. Set the grilled kabobs on the greens and drizzle a little aïoli over each one. Serve immediately.

BLT on a Stick

Toothpicks ave necessary to hold together these cocktail BLTs from Gordon's House of Fine Eats, on Florida Street in San Francisco.

> 2 slices bacon
> 2 slices square white sandwich bread, crusts
>   removed
> 1 tablespoon mayonnaise
> Black pepper in a mill
> 1 slice of iceberg lettuce, 4 inches by 4 inches by
>   1¼ inch thick
> 4 ripe cherry tomatoes, preferably Sweet 100s

Fry the bacon until it is just crisp and drain on a brown paper bag. Cut the ends of the bacon so that the slices are perfectly straight. Cut each piece into four 1-inch squares. Set aside.

Toast the bread until it is golden brown. Spread half the mayonnaise on both pieces of toast, and grind a little pepper on top. Set the lettuce on one piece of toast, and trim the edges to make an exact fit. Cut the toast with the lettuce into four equal squares. Cut the second piece of toast into squares of the same size.

Put one of the toast-and-lettuce squares on a toothpick, with the lettuce facing up. Add a piece of bacon, pressing it down onto the lettuce. Add a tomato, another piece of bacon, and a second piece of toast, mayonnaise side down. Repeat until four squares have been made. Serve immediately.

Stuffed Cherry Tomatoes

These little morsels are easiest to make with large cherry tomatoes. Many varieties yield fruit nearly the size of Ping-Pong balls; look for them at your farmers' market.

> 10 slices bacon
> 36 ripe cherry tomatoes
> 3 cups finely shredded iceberg lettuce, outer leaves only
> 3 tablespoons minced fresh cilantro
> ⅓ cup Lime-Jalapeño Mayonnaise (page 127), thinned with a little hot water, in a squeeze bottle
> ¼ cup Toasted Bread Crumbs (page 138)

Fry the bacon until crisp, drain on a brown paper bag, and mince.

Using a tomato knife or sharp paring knife, cut off the stem core of each tomato, slicing just above the shoulder. Use a very small spoon to scoop out and discard the seeds and gel of each tomato.

In a medium bowl, mix together the lettuce, cilantro, and minced bacon and fill each tomato with about a teaspoonful. Squeeze a little mayonnaise into each tomato and top with bread crumbs. Spread the remaining lettuce mixture on a serving platter, set the stuffed tomatoes on top, and serve immediately.

Bacon and Tomato Galettes with Aïoli

M ake the pastry and roll out the dough the day before serving. Then you can quickly finish up lovely free-form tarts, perfect for lunch or cocktails.

For the Pastry
2 cups all-purpose flour
¾ teaspoon kosher salt
12 tablespoons (1½ sticks) unsalted butter, cold, or
    a mixture of butter and bacon fat
½ cup ice-cold water

For the Filling
3 slices bacon
2½ cups (about 1½ pints) sliced cherry tomatoes
2 garlic cloves, minced
2 tablespoons snipped fresh chives
Kosher salt
Black pepper in a mill
4 ounces (1 cup) grated artisan Cheddar, such as
    Montgomery
1 egg white, mixed with 1 tablespoon water
3 tablespoons Aïoli (pages 128–131), thinned with a
    little lemon juice

First, prepare the pastry. Combine the flour and salt in a medium bowl. Cut in the butter, using your fingers or a pastry cutter, until the mixture resembles cornmeal. Work very quickly so the butter does not become too warm. Add ice water and press the dough together gently until it just comes together; do not overmix. Press the dough into a ball, wrap it tightly in plastic wrap, and refrigerate for at least 30 minutes.

Line two baking sheets with parchment paper and set aside. Cut the dough into 2 pieces and cut each piece into 6 smaller pieces. Place the dough on a floured work surface and, using the palm of your hand, pat it flat. Roll the dough into a circle about ⅛ inch thick and about 5 inches in diameter.

Set the pastry circles on the baking sheet, cover lightly, and keep in the refrigerator until ready to fill..

Fry the bacon until almost crisp, drain on a brown paper bag, and dice. To prepare the filling, combine the tomatoes, garlic, and chives in a medium bowl and toss gently but thoroughly. Season with salt and pepper.

Preheat the oven to 400°F.

Divide the cheese among the pastry circles, spreading it out, but leaving a 1-inch margin of pastry. Spoon some of the filling on top of the cheese. Scatter bacon on top of the tomatoes.

Gently fold the edges of the pastry up and over the filling, pleating the edges as you fold. Brush the edges with the egg wash and bake until the pastry is golden brown, about 30 minutes.

Transfer to a rack to cool until warm. Drizzle a swirl of aïoli on top of each galette and serve immediately.

Bruschetta

In the past decade, bruschetta has become enormously popular; not just in restaurants but in homes around the country. This BLT version makes a light summer lunch.

> 6 slices bacon
> 6 large garlic cloves
> 1½ pounds ripe tomatoes, peeled, seeded
>   (pages 132–33), and diced
> 1 tablespoon minced fresh herbs
> Kosher salt
> Black pepper in a mill
> ¼ cup extra virgin olive oil
> ⅓ cup mayonnaise
> 1 tablespoon fresh lemon juice
> 1 tablespoon hot water
> 2 quarts oak-leaf lettuce leaves, rinsed
>   and dried
> Half a 1-pound loaf country-style
>   Italian bread

Fry the bacon, turning once, until it is crisp. Drain on a brown paper bag. Mince it and set aside.

Mince two cloves of garlic, mix them with the tomatoes and herbs, season with salt and pepper, and stir in the olive oil. Set aside.

In a small bowl, combine the mayonnaise, lemon juice, and hot water. Put one of the remaining garlic cloves through a press and stir the purée into the mayonnaise. Cover and set aside.

Spread the lettuce evenly over individual plates.

Cut the bread into eight slices and toast them. Cut the 3 remaining garlic cloves in half and rub each slice of toast on one side with a piece of garlic, pressing the cut side into the bread. As you finish rubbing the toast with garlic, set it on the lettuce, two pieces per serving.

Serve immediately, setting the tomatoes, the bacon, and the mayonnaise in the center of the table. Guests assemble the bruschetta themselves, spooning some of the tomato mixture on top of the bread, followed by some bacon and a drizzle of mayonnaise.

BLT Napoleons

At first glance this recipe may seem—and, certainly, it sounds—silly, but the way in which the flavors and textures mingle are really quite good. And it's an excellent way to sneak the humble BLT into an elegant dinner party.

1 to 2 tablespoons butter, melted
12 puff pastry rectangles, 2½ inches by 4 inches each
6 slices bacon
6 ounces *fromage blanc* or fresh ricotta
½ cup Tomato Concassé (page 132)
Kosher salt
Black pepper in a mill
1 cup finely shredded iceberg lettuce, outer leaves
   only
3 tablespoons Lemon Zest Mayonnaise (page 127)
½ cup currant tomatoes, cut in half

Preheat the oven to 375°F. Line a baking sheet with a nonstick mat or brush it with a little of the melted butter. Set the puff pastry rectangles on the baking sheet, brush the tops with melted butter, and bake until they are puffed and golden brown, about 12 minutes.

Dice the bacon, then fry until just crisp. Drain on a brown paper bag.

Warm four individual salad plates. Set a cooked pastry rectangle on each plate and top it with some of the *fromage blanc,* scattering or dotting the cheese over the surface of the pastry. Spoon about a tablespoon of tomato concassé on top of each rectangle, season with salt and pepper, and scatter a little bacon on top. Set a second rectangle of pastry on top, divide the remaining cheese evenly among the servings, spoon some of the remaining tomato concassé on top, and add some of the remaining diced bacon. Top with a remaining pastry rectangle.

Set a small mound of shredded lettuce on top of each serving and spoon a little mayonnaise on top. Scatter currant tomatoes over each napoleon, and serve immediately.

Soups

Butter Lettuce Soup with Bacon and Tomato

SERVES 4

The colors of this soup sparkle like jewels, a shimmering that lingers on the palate. If you grow lettuce or buy it from the farmers' market, use the entire head. If you use supermarket lettuce, remove the tough outer leaves.

2 tablespoons olive oil
1 yellow onion, diced
2 large heads butter lettuce, cored, washed, dried
Kosher salt
Black pepper in a mill
3 tablespoons minced fresh flat-leaf parsley
4 cups homemade Chicken Broth (page 140)
4 slices bacon
1 cup fresh tomato juice, from Tomato Concassé
    (see headnote, page 132)
3 tablespoons extra virgin olive oil
2 tablespoons snipped chives
½ cup currant tomatoes, mixed colors, halved
4 tablespoons crème fraîche

Heat the olive oil in a medium soup pot set over medium-low heat, add the onion, and sauté until soft and fragrant, about 15 minutes.

Meanwhile, cut the lettuce into ⅜-inch-wide slices. Stir it into the cooked onions, season with salt and pepper, add the parsley, and pour in the chicken broth. Increase the heat to medium high, bring the broth to a boil, reduce the heat to low, and simmer for 7 minutes.

Dice the bacon and cook until it is crisp; transfer onto a brown paper bag to drain.

Using an immersion blender, purée the soup.

To serve hot, heat the tomato juice. Ladle the soup into warm soup plates. Drizzle the tomato juice in concentric circles over the soup, and drizzle the olive oil in a similar pattern. Scatter minced bacon, snipped chives, and currant tomatoes on top, add a dollop of crème fraîche, and serve immediately.

VARIATION: To serve the soup chilled, refrigerate the soup and the tomato juice, covered, for 2 to 3 hours before assembling and garnishing as above.

Spicy Tomato Soup with Bacon and Lettuce

SERVES 6

There is a moment, usually in late August, when the California landscape is suddenly bathed in gold. As hot as it may be, fall is in the air. Like the trees whose leaves begin to fall and the cats whose coats become thicker, our bodies know winter is on its way. We might not have wanted soup in July, even when it was cold, but we want it now. This soup serves that longing, yet evokes summer's first BLT, too.

> 4 pounds ripe slicing tomatoes, peeled, seeded, and
>   chopped
> ¼ pound bacon (about 4 slices)
> 1 yellow onion, minced
> 6 garlic cloves, minced
> 1 or 2 serrano chiles, minced
> Kosher salt
> Black pepper in a mill
> 2 cups Strong Chicken Broth (page 141)
> 6 thick slices country-style bread
> 3 garlic cloves
> 5 cups shredded romaine lettuce
> ⅓ cup Aïoli (pages 128–131)

Place the tomatoes in a strainer lined with cheesecloth and set over a deep container, and let them drain for 20 minutes. Reserve the strained liquid to thin the soup.

Fry the bacon in a large soup pot over medium heat until it is almost completely crisp. Transfer the bacon onto a brown paper bag to drain; pour off all but 3 tablespoons of the bacon fat in the pot. Reduce the heat to medium low and sauté the onion until very soft and fragrant, about 20 minutes. Add the garlic and serranos and sauté 2 minutes more. Season with salt and pepper.

Stir in the broth and the drained tomatoes, bring to a boil over medium heat, and simmer for 15 minutes. Thin with liquid from the tomatoes, if necessary for consistency. Correct the seasoning.

Crumble the bacon.

Toast the bread until it is deep golden brown. Cut the garlic in half lengthwise and rub one side of each piece of toast with a piece of garlic, pressing the cut side into the bread.

Divide the shredded romaine among individual soup bowls and ladle the hot soup over it. Sprinkle crumbled bacon over each portion, and top with a spoonful of aïoli. Set the bowls on plates, add a piece of toast, and serve immediately.

Potato Soup with Tomatoes and Bacon

SERVES 4 TO 6

This soup will get you through the barren months of no fresh tomatoes, when it is impossible to make a good BLT. You can, if you want, top the soup with a flurry of shredded lettuce to add that appealing contrast of temperature and texture.

3 slices bacon
1 tablespoon extra virgin olive oil
1 yellow onion, diced
6 garlic cloves, minced
Kosher salt
Black pepper in a mill
4 to 5 medium Yukon Gold potatoes, scrubbed and
    sliced
3 cups homemade Chicken Broth (page 140)
One 28-ounce can diced tomatoes, with their juice
4 tablespoons minced fresh flat-leaf parsley or fresh
    snipped chives
Aïoli (pages 128–131), optional

Fry the bacon in a heavy soup pot until it is crisp, transfer it onto a brown paper bag to drain, and pour off all but a tablespoon of the bacon fat from the pot. Add the olive oil, return the pot to medium-low heat, add the onion, and cook until it is soft and fragrant, about 12 minutes. Add the garlic, sauté 2 minutes more, and season with salt and pepper.

Add the potatoes, chicken broth, and 3 cups of water. Bring to a boil over high heat, reduce the heat to medium low, and simmer until the potatoes are nearly tender, about 15 minutes. Add the tomatoes and their juice and simmer 10 minutes more.

Purée the soup with an immersion blender, adding more water if necessary for a proper soup consistency. Stir in 3 tablespoons of the parsley, taste the soup, and correct the seasoning. Crumble the bacon.

Ladle into soup bowls, sprinkle some of the bacon and some of the remaining parsley on top, and garnish with a spoonful of aïoli, if using. Serve immediately.

This soup is excellent reheated, and can be kept in the refrigerator for 3 to 4 days.

Watercress Soup with Currant Tomato Salsa and Bacon

Watercress wilts and and begins to decay quickly, so be sure yours is absolutely fresh before beginning this tangy soup.

For the Salsa

1½ cups yellow, red, and orange currant or cherry
        tomatoes, halved or quartered
2 tablespoons minced red onion
1 large garlic clove, minced
1 serrano chile, minced
1 tablespoon fresh lime juice
2 tablespoons extra virgin olive oil
1 tablespoon minced watercress or peppercress
1 tablespoon minced cilantro
Kosher salt
Black pepper in a mill

For the Soup

2 tablespoons salt, plus more to taste
¾ pound watercress, largest stems discarded
4 slices bacon
2 tablespoons olive oil

1 leek, white and pale green parts only, very thinly
    sliced and thoroughly rinsed
2 garlic cloves, minced
1 large (¾ pound) potato, peeled and thinly sliced
Kosher salt
5 cups Chicken Broth (page 140), or water
½ cup minced fresh flat-leaf parsley
Black pepper in a mill

First, make the salsa. In a medium bowl, toss together the tomatoes, onion, garlic, and serrano. Stir in the lime juice and olive
oil, add the watercress and the cilantro, and season with salt and
pepper. Taste, correct the seasoning, and set aside, covered.

Fill a large bowl one-third full with ice and add water until the
bowl is half full. Fill a large pot half full with water, add the 2
tablespoons salt, and bring to a boil over high heat. Add the
watercress, stir, and when the water returns to a boil, quickly
transfer the cress to the ice water. Submerge for 2 minutes,
remove the cress, squeeze out all of the water, and set on a tea
towel to continue to drain.

Fry the bacon until crisp. Reserve 1 tablespoon of the fat and
transfer the bacon onto a brown paper bag to drain.

Heat the reserved bacon fat and olive oil in a medium pot set
over medium-low heat, add the leek, and sauté until soft and
wilted, about 10 minutes. Add the garlic, sauté 2 minutes more,
add the potato, stir, and season with salt.

Add the chicken broth, increase the heat to medium, and simmer until the potato is tender, about 10 to 12 minutes. Stir in the blanched watercress and the parsley and simmer 2 minutes. Season with black pepper, taste, and correct the seasoning. Remove the soup from the heat and purée with an immersion blender or in a conventional blender.

Pour through a medium strainer or sieve into a warm soup tureen. Garnish the soup with a swirl of crème fraîche and the tomato salsa. Crumble the bacon, scatter it on top, and serve immediately.

BLTs

The Classic BLT

MAKES I SANDWICH

There is great variation among BLTs; with so few ingredients, each one is crucial. The tomato is trickiest. If your BLT jones is an effect of pregnancy, buy tomatoes attached to a segment of vine; you can find them year-round. Slice them, sprinkle a little kosher salt over them, and let them sit. The flavor will perk up a bit. If your craving is simple lust, wait until local tomatoes appear in your farmers' market. Early Girls are among the first to ripen; as the season gets under way, use your favorite varieties. For lettuce, remove the first outer leaf and then use only the next three layers. Further in, iceberg lettuce gets a little cabbagey. You need the color and delicacy of those outer leaves.

2 slices bacon
2 slices white sandwich bread
1 to 2 tablespoons mayonnaise
1 ripe tomato, cored and cut into 5-mm
    (not quite ¼-inch) rounds
Kosher salt
Black pepper in a mill
3 iceberg lettuce leaves

Cut the bacon slices in half crosswise, fry until crisp, and drain on a brown paper bag. Shortly before the bacon is fully cooked,

toast the bread in a conventional toaster until it is golden brown over about a third to a half of its surface. If you prefer darker toast, let it cook a bit longer, though if it is too dark, its taste will eclipse other flavors.

Spread mayonnaise on both pieces of bread, using as much or as little as you like. Arrange the tomato slices on one piece of bread, overlapping them slightly, and season them lightly with salt and pepper. Set the bacon on top of the tomatoes. Put the lettuce on top, add the second piece of bread, mayonnaise side down, and cut in half diagonally. Enjoy immediately.

VARIATIONS

When sweet onions are in season, add a ⅛-inch-thick slice on top of the mayonnaise and under the tomatoes.

Hate mayonnaise? Drizzle a good extra virgin olive oil over the bread after it toasts and top it with a thin layer of *fromage blanc* or fresh ricotta before adding the tomatoes.

Easily bored? Use a flavored mayonnaise (pages 125–127) after you've had your fill of the traditional version.

The FTBBLT: The Full-Tilt Boogie BLT

The inspiration for this sandwich comes from several sources, a confession from Virginia Watkins of Niman Ranch that she likes to smear a little bacon fat on the bread of her BLTs, a story from a friend about the secret ingredient (bacon fat, of course) in her mother's biscuits, and a tip from Adam Rapaport, a senior editor of *GQ* magazine, that Chat 'n Chew, near Union Square in New York City, makes the baconiest BLT around, stacking it up on seven-grain bread like pastrami.

8 slices dry-cured bacon, cut in half crosswise
2 center-cut slices soft country-style bread
¼ cup mayonnaise
3 slices ripe beefsteak tomato, preferably Black
    Brandywine
Kosher salt
Black pepper in a mill
6 to 8 leaves very fresh oak-leaf lettuce

Preheat the oven to 400°F. Fry the bacon in a large frying pan until it is just crisp, transfer it onto a brown paper bag, and let it drain. Pour off enough of the bacon fat so that there is about ⅛ inch left in the pan. While the bacon is frying, toast the bread in

the oven until it is golden brown over a quarter of its surface. Do not let it darken more than this.

Set the frying pan with the bacon fat over medium-high heat. Put the bread in the frying pan, matching the pieces so that what will be the inside of the sandwich is face down in the fat. Fry until the bread is evenly browned, about 5 or 6 minutes. Use tongs to transfer the bread to a work surface, setting it fried side up.

Spread mayonnaise over both pieces of bread. Arrange the tomato slices on one piece, season with a little salt and pepper, and stack the bacon on top, as you might layer pastrami. Set the oak-leaf lettuce on the bacon, and top with the remaining slice of bread, mayonnaise side down. Cut in half, set on several layers of paper towels, and enjoy immediately.

National BLT Month

In 2000, the National Pork Producers Council declared April to be National BLT Month, an effort at counterseasonal retail promotion. By 2002, the council, realizing that you can't make a good BLT until tomatoes are in season, expanded the campaign to something called "Better with Bacon," a retail promotion lasting from April to October. To celebrate the BLT in April, start seeds indoors or set out seedlings, depending on where you live.

The SBAT

Eateries in California tend to offer avocado on virtually everything, from sandwiches and burritos to black bean soup and pizza. With the abundance of delicious Hass avocados in the state, natives don't find the offer strange, but visitors often shake their heads and mutter "California!" under their breath. Mustard has no place on a traditional BLT, but it is delicious with avocado.

> 2 slices bacon, cut in half crosswise
> 1 tablespoon mayonnaise
> 2 teaspoons Dijon mustard
> Black pepper in a mill
> 2 slices San Francisco sourdough bread
> 4 lengthwise slices firm-ripe avocado
> 1 ripe tomato, sliced
> Kosher salt
> Small handful (about ½ cup) mustard sprouts or
>   onion sprouts

Fry the bacon until it is just crisp and drain it on a brown paper bag. In a small bowl, mix together the mayonnaise and mustard and season with black pepper.

Toast or grill the bread lightly and spread some of the mayonnaise and mustard mixture over both slices. Set the sliced avocado on top of one slice of bread, set the tomatoes on top, and sprinkle with a little salt. Top with the bacon and sprouts and enjoy immediately.

The PAT

Pancetta is unsmoked salt-cured pork belly. An essential ingredient in many Italian dishes, it can be found almost everywhere in the United States. Look for it at deli counters, and ask that it be sliced thin but not paper thin. A PAT is more delicate than a BLT, just the thing on a hot day.

3 to 4 thin slices pancetta
2 slices Italian hearth bread
3 tablespoons Aïoli (pages 128–131)
1 ripe tomato, sliced
Kosher salt
A handful of arugula

Sauté the pancetta until it is just crisp. Toast or grill the bread until it is golden brown. Spread aïoli over both pieces of bread. Arrange the tomato slices on top of one piece and sprinkle with kosher salt. Set the pancetta on top, breaking the strips in half if necessary to make them fit. Set a handful of arugula on top of the pancetta and top with the remaining slices of bread, aïoli side down, of course. Cut in half and enjoy immediately.

BLTS on the Menu

Throughout America, you'll find inventive versions of our finest sandwich, some featuring a local specialty, others highlighting a chef's creativity. Here's a selection:

— *Lobster BLT Pizza with a Dijon Crust*
and Smoked Provolone —
The Bound'ry Restaurant, Nashville, Tennessee

— *Salmon BLT* —
Café Lolo, Santa Rosa, California

— *Open-faced BLTs with Grilled Soft-Shell Crab*
and Basil Mayonnaise —
Doris & Ed's, Highlands, New Jersey

— *Lobster BLT* —
Eagan's, Minneapolis

— *Foie Gras BLT* —
Fearrington House Restaurant, Chapel Hill, North
Carolina

— *Crab BLT with Basil Mustard Mayonnaise* —
Gordon Biersch Restaurant, Tempe, Arizona

— *Lobster BLT* —
Grand Central Station Oyster Bar, New York City

— *BLT on a Baguette, with Hobbs Bacon* —
Hayes Street Grill at the Ferry Plaza Farmers' Market,
San Francisco

— The World's Smallest BLTs —
Inn at Little Washington, Virginia

— Crab BLT —
Kelly's Mission Rock, San Francisco

— Soft–Shell Crab BLT —
L'Uraku, Honolulu

— Lobster BLT Wrap with Tomato–Lemon Mayonnaise
—
Mims, Syosset, New York

— Cornmeal–Crusted Soft–Shell Crab BLT
with Rémoulade —
Moose's, North Beach, San Francisco

— Smoked Maine Lobster Club with Bacon, Arugula,
and Tomato —
Postrio, San Francisco

— Dungeness Crab BLT on Toasted Focaccia —
Seafood Peddler, San Rafael

— Lobster BLT with Tarragon and Lemon Mayonnaise
and Grilled Ciabatta —
Terra Restaurant & Bar, San Diego

— Seared Tuna BLT with Wasabi Mayonnaise —
Zoë, New York City

The BSLT

At Pike Place Market in Seattle, there's a stand that offers wonderful salmon sandwiches. I particularly enjoy them for breakfast, when the market is not crowded and the air is crisp and sharp. I've used that sandwich as inspiration for a BLT with salmon. The order in which you assemble this sandwich is crucial, so be sure to follow directions.

⅓ cup mayonnaise, or Smoky Romesco Sauce
    (page 136)
2 tablespoons minced fresh basil
2 garlic cloves, crushed and minced
Black pepper in a mill
Kosher salt
4 slices bacon, cut in half crosswise
4 pieces fresh wild salmon belly (see Note)
4 soft rolls
2 ripe slicing tomatoes, cored and sliced
8 inner butter lettuce leaves, torn into bite-sized pieces

In a small bowl, combine the mayonnaise, basil, and garlic. Season very generously with black pepper, taste, and season with salt if needed. Cover and set aside.

Fry the bacon until it is crisp and transfer onto a brown paper bag to drain. Heat a nonstick sauté pan over medium heat, season the salmon on both sides with salt and pepper, sauté it for 3 minutes, turn, and sauté for 2 minutes more. Remove from the heat.

Quickly toast the rolls until golden brown. Spread mayonnaise on the bottom half of each roll. Arrange 3 slices of tomatoes on top, season lightly with salt, set two pieces of bacon on the tomatoes, and put the salmon on top of the bacon. Add some of the lettuce and cover with the top half of the roll. Serve the sandwiches immediately.

NOTE: According to the Seafood Watch guide published by the Monterey Bay Aquarium, all farmed salmon—Atlantic salmon and farmed Pacific king salmon—should be avoided entirely. The effects of salmon farming on the ocean environment is devastating, and the salmon themselves are of questionable nutritional value. Farmed salmon are fed beef by-products, chemical dyes, hormones, and antibiotics. They contain significantly less omega-3 fatty acids, the nutrients that make the fish so good for us, than wild salmon. Salmon farms also have had a disastrous impact on domestic fishermen. With a glut of farmed salmon from Chile, British Columbia, and Norway on the market, our fishermen are struggling to break even with today's low wholesale price, less than a third of what it was in the late 1980s.

Wild salmon populations on the West Coast of the United States are carefully monitored, and salmon fishing is allowed only when populations are abundant. You can usually find excellent wild king salmon from the beginning of May through September and sometimes October. Some fishermen are beginning to sell their catch at farmers' markets. If you're not sure if a fish is wild, be sure to ask.

When wild salmon is not available, don't revert to the farmed fish; instead, enjoy the species that are in season and listed as "Best Choices" on the Seafood Watch guide (mbayaq.org).

Crescent BLTs

Evelyn Cheatham is one of the most gifted chefs and talented teachers in the country. Yet, instead of enjoying the limelight, she teaches at-risk youths how to cook and how to savor the pleasures of the table. During her tenure at a probation facility for young teenagers, the kids often asked for these "crescent sandwiches." The capers are my own flourish; I like their tangy contrast with the sweet dried tomatoes.

> 6 slices bacon, cut in half crosswise
> 4 croissants
> ⅓ cup Dried-Tomato Mayonnaise (page 127)
> 1 tablespoon capers, optional
> 3 to 4 small slicing tomatoes, sliced
> Kosher salt
> 2 cups shredded romaine lettuce

Preheat the oven to 325°F. Fry the bacon until it is crisp and transfer it onto a brown paper bag to drain. Cut the croissants in half lengthwise and set them in the oven until they are heated through, 7 to 8 minutes.

Spread a generous tablespoonful of mayonnaise over the bottom half of each croissant, scatter with capers, if using, and top with several slices of tomato. Season with salt, set 3 pieces of bacon on top of the tomatoes, and add a handful of shredded lettuce. Top with other half of the croissant and serve immediately.

Focaccia BLT

Focaccia makes an excellent BLT, especially when it is fresh and hot. Buy your focaccia from a good bakery; the kind wrapped in plastic and available in supermarkets is always disappointing.

1 focaccia square, 10 inches by 10 inches, cut into
    4 equal pieces
6 slices bacon, cut in half crosswise
3 tablespoons Olive Mayonnaise (page 127),
    optional
2 medium ripe slicing tomatoes, cored and cut in
    ¼-inch-thick slices
Kosher salt
Black pepper in a mill
2 tablespoons extra virgin olive oil, optional
3 generous handfuls arugula or oak-leaf lettuce

Preheat the oven to 325°F and toast the focaccia until it begins to color on its edges, about 7 to 8 minutes.

Meanwhile, fry the bacon in a medium sauté pan until it is crisp and transfer it onto a brown paper bag to drain.

Set the hot focaccia on a work surface and spread mayonnaise, if using, over the top of each piece. If not, cover two of the pieces with tomato slices, season with a little salt and pepper, and drizzle with some of the olive oil. Set the bacon on top, add some of the arugula, and top with the remaining pieces of focaccia, smeared with mayonnaise if using. Cut the sandwiches in half diagonally and serve immediately.

Fisherman's BLT

If you've never tried sand dab, consider using it in this sandwich. It is one of the most delicious fish around, though surprisingly, it has never become popular outside of the San Francisco Bay Area. Yet sand dabs are abundant in California's coastal waters, easy to prepare, and inexpensive. Sand dabs are on the Monterey Bay Aquarium's Seafood Watch Best Choices list, too; sole—petrale, Dover, and English—is on the "Proceed with Caution" list.

Preheat the pan before cooking these fish fillets so they will be pleasantly crisp.

4 slices bacon, cut in half crosswise
½ cup all-purpose flour
Kosher salt
Black pepper in a mill
½ teaspoon chipotle powder
4 boned flatfish fillets, such as petrale sole, about
    6 ounces each
4 rolls, such as Portuguese rolls or country-style
    round sourdough rolls, split
½ cup Caper Mayonnaise (page 126), Rémoulade
    Sauce (page 134), or Chipotle Mayonnaise
    (page 127)

2 or 3 medium tomatoes, cored and sliced
4 large iceberg lettuce leaves, broken in half

Fry the bacon in a large sauté pan until it is crisp, transfer it onto a brown paper bag to drain, and pour off all but 3 tablespoons of the bacon fat from the pan. Set the pan aside.

Put the flour on a plate, season generously with salt and pepper, add the chipotle powder, and mix with a fork. Press each fish fillet into the flour, turning to coat it thoroughly. Shake off excess flour.

Toast the rolls lightly in the oven. Spread mayonnaise over both pieces of each roll. Cover the bottom half of each roll with tomatoes and set 2 pieces of bacon on top of each.

Reheat the bacon fat in the skillet until it is hot but not smoking. Fry the fillets, turning once, until they are golden brown on both sides, about 6 to 7 minutes total cooking time. Set a fillet on top of each sandwich. Divide the lettuce among the sandwiches, setting it on top of the fish fillet. Set the top half of the rolls on the sandwiches and serve immediately.

The Club

Whenever my friend John checks into a hotel, he orders a club sandwich. "As we all know, room service food can be dreadful," he says, "but a club sandwich is almost always good, especially when it's made with real roasted turkey." His favorite is served at the Mauna Kea Resort Hotel.

Although a club is a BLT with an extra layer, there is dispute over which came first. But whether it was the inspiration for a bigger sandwich or the deconstruction of a complex one, the BLT is a study in delicious simplicity. The more elaborate club is a perfect place to let your imagination rip: apply everything you know about building a perfect BLT, then add a second layer based on seasonality and passion. To be absolutely traditional, you'll want to omit the fresh sage leaves—I use them because I like them with roasted turkey, and because they grow right outside my kitchen door—and serve potato chips and a dill pickle alongside.

2 slices bacon, cut in half lengthwise
3 slices good white sandwich bread
2 tablespoons mayonnaise
1 ripe tomato, sliced
Kosher salt
2 or 3 romaine lettuce leaves

4 fresh sage leaves (optional)
3 slices turkey, preferably freshly roasted
Black pepper in a mill

Fry the bacon until it is crisp and drain it on a brown paper bag.

Toast the bread until it is golden brown. Spread mayonnaise on one side each of two slices of bread. Arrange the tomatoes on top of one slice and sprinkle lightly with salt. Set the bacon on top of the tomatoes and set the lettuce on top of the bacon. Spread mayonnaise on both sides of the remaining piece of bread and set that on top of the lettuce. Arrange the sage leaves on top, add the turkey, season with salt and pepper, and top with the last piece of bread, mayonnaise side down.

VARIATIONS   Omit the turkey and the sage leaf, and use the suggested mayonnaise for the entire sandwich, not just the top layer.

Seared foie gras with Balsamic Mayonnaise (page 126)

Smoked trout fillet with Chipotle Mayonnaise (page 127)

Fresh crabmeat with Smoky Romesco Sauce (page 136)

Salmon with Herb Mayonnaise (page 127)

Lobster with Caviar Mayonnaise (page 127)

Fried oysters with Aïoli (pages 128–131)

The SSLT

Fried salmon skin is popular in trendy sushi bars, where it is tucked into rolls and tossed into salads with miso dressing. When cooked until crisp, it is wonderful and not unlike bacon. If you don't want bacon or just happen to have good salmon around, use strips of skin fried to a crisp for a wonderful SSLT.

> 4 slices bread, lightly toasted
> 3 tablespoons Lemon Zest Mayonnaise (page 127)
> 1 to 2 ripe tomatoes, cored and sliced
> Kosher salt
> Black pepper in a mill
> 6 salmon skin strips, ¾ inch wide by 4 inches long,
>   fried until crisp (see Note)
> 2 handfuls oak-leaf lettuce

Set the bread on a work surface and spread mayonnaise on one side of each piece. Arrange 3 or 4 slices of tomato on two of the pieces of bread and season with salt and pepper. Set 3 pieces of salmon skin across each layer of tomatoes, top with a handful of lettuce and a remaining piece of bread, mayonnaise side down, of course. Cut in half diagonally and serve immediately.

NOTE: To use salmon skin in this recipe, be certain that the salmon has been scaled. It is easier to remove the skin from cooked salmon, so the best time to make these sandwiches is the day after you've roasted or grilled a salmon. Pull the skin from the salmon, removing all attached flesh. Cut it into crosswise pieces ¾ inch wide and either fry in a nonstick pan or broil under a gas flame, turning once, until it is very crisp.

The Soft-Shell Crab BLT

Susan Goss, who is chef and co-owner, with her husband Drew, of the popular Zinfandel Restaurant in Chicago, says her favorite way to enjoy soft-shell crabs is in a BLT, this one, to be exact. "Although this looks elegant served open face," she explains in an e-mail, "the sheer joy of eating all those wonderful flavors together makes a closed sandwich, cut in half, the way to go. The crispy crab, smoky bacon, juicy sweet tomatoes, soft lettuces, and spicy rémoulade make this one sandwich you will never forget!"

2 or 3 thick slices bacon

2 slices American farmhouse cracked wheat bread

Olive oil

2 to 3 tablespoons Rémoulade Sauce (page 134)

Handful of soft organic greens (such as oak-leaf and butter lettuces), tossed with a little vinaigrette

3 to 4 tomato slices

Oil for deep frying

1 medium soft-shell crab, cleaned

½ cup seasoned all-purpose flour (see Note)

Fry the bacon until it is crisp, transfer it onto a brown paper bag, and let it drain.

Heat a stove-top grill. Brush the bread on both sides with olive oil and grill it until it is golden brown. Spread rémoulade on one side of both pieces of bread. Set the greens on top of the rémoulade on one slice of bread and arrange the tomato slices on top. Set the bacon on top of the tomatoes.

Pour 2 inches of oil into a medium saucepan or frying pan and set it over medium heat until it is hot, but not smoking, about 345°F. Dust the soft-shell crab with the seasoned flour, shake off any excess, and carefully submerge the crab into the hot oil. Fry for 1 minute, transfer onto a brown paper bag, and let drain briefly.

Put the fried crab on top of the bacon, set the remaining piece of bread, rémoulade side down, on top, cut the sandwich in half, and enjoy immediately.

NOTE: To season the flour, add 2 teaspoons of kosher salt, several turns of black pepper, and a teaspoon of good paprika. Mix with a fork and put in a wide, shallow dish.

The ZLT

When zucchini is perfectly grilled, it has a thin, almost gossamer coating. If the heat is too high, the zucchini will burn before the coating forms; if it is too low, the zucchini will become mushy. It might take practice to get it perfect, but in August and September, there's more than enough zucchini for a few mistakes.

¼ cup mayonnaise
2 teaspoons fresh lemon juice
¼ teaspoon chipotle powder
Black pepper in a mill
1 medium zucchini, 5 to 6 inches long, washed
    and trimmed
Kosher salt
Olive oil
1 focaccia square, 10 inches by 10 inches, cut into
    4 equal pieces
1 medium or 2 small ripe slicing tomatoes, cored
    and cut into ¼-inch-thick slices
4 to 6 fresh basil leaves
8 to 10 medium romaine lettuce leaves, shredded

In a small bowl, combine the mayonnaise, lemon juice, chipotle powder, and several turns of black pepper. Cover and set aside.

Preheat the oven to 325°F. Cut the zucchini lengthwise into thin (⅛-inch) strips; this is best done on a mandoline. Heat a stove-top grill or ridged cast-iron pan. Season the zucchini on both sides with salt, and brush a little olive oil over each slice. Grill the zucchini, turning several times, until it is tender and shows even grill marks and a slight crust on both sides. While the zucchini is cooking, heat the focaccia until it just begins to color on its edges.

Set the focaccia on a work surface and spread mayonnaise over the top of each piece. Cover two of the pieces with tomato slices, season with a little salt, and top with zucchini slices. Arrange the basil leaves on top of the zucchini, season with several turns of black pepper, add some of the lettuce, and top with the remaining pieces of bread, mayonnaise side down. Serve immediately.

The VLT

Vegetarians can readily enjoy the spirit, if not the letter, of a BLT, but not by using a commercial or homemade substitute that tries to mimic the flavor and texture of real bacon. Better to find natural ingredients that contribute some of the characteristics—here, the salt and the crunch—with their own good qualities. For a smoky flourish, use Chipotle Mayonnaise (page 127).

For the crisp leeks
**6 medium leeks, white and pale green parts only,
       thoroughly cleaned and dried**
½ cup all-purpose flour
2 to 3 cups mild olive oil, or other neutral oil
Kosher salt
Black pepper in a mill

For the sandwich
1 whole wheat sourdough roll, split
**2 tablespoons Herb Mayonnaise (page 127) with
       fines herbes**
1 ripe tomato, sliced
Kosher salt
Black pepper in a mill
**2 medium butter lettuce leaves, from the middle of
       the head**

First, prepare the leeks. Cut them into very thin rounds and check them to be sure there is no dirt or sand hiding in any of the layers. Put them in a medium bowl, sprinkle the flour over them, and toss thoroughly. Set aside.

Pour the oil into a medium saucepan; there should be at least 2½ inches of oil in the pan; if there isn't, add enough to bring the oil to that level. Set the saucepan over medium-high heat until it reaches 350°F. Add a handful of sliced leeks and use cooking sticks or chopsticks to separate the leeks and prevent them from sticking together. Fry until they are golden brown and crisp, but not burned. Use a long-handled strainer to transfer them onto a brown paper bag to drain. Continue until all of the leeks have been fried. Season with salt and pepper, tossing the cooked leeks gently but thoroughly. Set aside a small handful for this sandwich, put the remainder into a container with a lid, and refrigerate for up to 5 days. (To reheat, spread on a baking sheet and bake at 350°F for 12 minutes.)

To make the sandwich, toast the roll in a 325°F oven, until it is heated through and just beginning to grow crisp on the cut sides.

Spread mayonnaise on both sides of the roll, and arrange tomato slices over the bottom half. Season with salt and pepper. Put a generous quantity of fried leeks on top of the tomatoes, add the lettuce leaves, and set the top piece of the roll over the lettuce, mayonnaise side down. Cut in half and enjoy immediately.

The VLT 2

Many years ago, an acquaintance offered me one of the simplest yet most delicious appetizers I've ever had, toasted nori dipped in a mixture of soy sauce and lime juice. It remains one of my favorite midnight snacks. Toasted nori makes an excellent substitute for bacon, too; it lacks the luscious fat of bacon, but provides crunch and an evocative whisper of salt.

2 teaspoons light (rice) miso
2 teaspoons fresh lemon juice, plus more to taste
2 tablespoons mild olive oil
2 slices organic multigrain bread
1 small to medium tomato
Kosher salt
Black pepper in a mill
½ sheet nori
3 fresh *shiso* leaves, if available
Small handful young *mizuna*

In a small bowl, mix together the miso, lemon juice, and olive oil. Taste the mixture, and add more lemon juice if needed for balance.

Toast the bread in a conventional toaster. Spread the miso "mayonnaise" over one side of both pieces of bread.

Remove the stem core of the tomato and cut it into ¼-inch-thick slices.

Arrange the tomato slices on top of one piece of bread and season lightly with salt and pepper.

Turn a gas or electric burner to high and carefully hold the nori over the heat until it crackles and shrinks, 15 to 20 seconds. Rotate it and turn it until the entire sheet is crisp. Tear it into pieces and arrange them over the tomatoes. Top with the *shiso* leaves, *mizuna*, and the remaining piece of bread, mayonnaise side down.

Cut the sandwich in half and enjoy immediately.

Pita BLT

Many pita sandwiches are made in half a pita opened like a pocket, which is easier to hold than one made with the whole pita but not as voluptuous. I like the sandwich as described here, but if you prefer to make it as a pocket, go ahead.

> 2 or 3 slices bacon, cut crosswise into 1-inch-wide
>   strips
> 3 or 4 large outer iceberg lettuce leaves
> 8 cherry tomatoes, cut in half crosswise
> 6 pitted black olives, cut in half
> 1 pita
> Kosher salt
> 3 tablespoons Olive Mayonnaise (page 127), or
>   mayonnaise of choice
> 1 tablespoon Toasted Bread Crumbs (page 138)

Preheat the oven to 325°F.

Cook the bacon in a heavy sauté pan until it is completely crisp. Transfer it onto a brown paper bag to drain.

Tear the lettuce into 1½-inch pieces.

Set the pita bread in the oven until it is heated through, about 5 minutes. Do not overcook; the bread should be soft and pliable.

Set the warm pita on a square of wax paper and set the lettuce in a mound in the center of the lower half of the bread. Scatter the tomatoes and olives on top and season lightly with salt. Scatter half the bacon over the lettuce and tomatoes and fold the pita into a loose cone. Wrap the wax paper around the lower half. Drizzle the mayonnaise over the top, add the remaining bacon and the bread crumbs and enjoy immediately.

VARIATION: If you have great backyard slicing tomatoes but no cherry tomatoes, cut one medium tomato into ¼-inch-thick rounds, cut the rounds in half, and use as directed.

Pita BCLT

Use whatever good crab you can get, blue crab from Maryland, peeky-toe crab, Dungeness crab, or any freshly cooked, chilled, and picked crabmeat.

> 2 slices bacon, cut crosswise into 1-inch-wide strips
> 3 or 4 large outer iceberg lettuce leaves
> Kosher salt
> 3 ounces fresh crabmeat, picked over for shells and cartilage
> 8 cherry tomatoes, cut in half crosswise
> 1 pita
> 2 to 3 tablespoons Rémoulade Sauce (page 134) or Smoky Romesco Sauce (page 136)
> 1 tablespoon Toasted Bread Crumbs (page 138)

Preheat the oven to 325°F.

Cook the bacon in a heavy sauté pan until it is completely crisp. Transfer it onto a brown paper bag to drain.

Tear the lettuce into 1½-inch pieces and season it lightly with salt.

Set the pita bread in the oven until it is heated through, about 5 minutes. Do not overcook; the bread should be soft and pliable.

Set the warm pita on a square of wax paper and set the lettuce in a mound in the center of the lower half of the bread. Top with the crab and scatter the tomatoes on top. Scatter half the bacon over the lettuce and tomatoes and fold the pita into a loose cone. Wrap the wax paper around the lower half. Drizzle the rémoulade sauce over the top, add the remaining bacon and the bread crumbs and enjoy immediately.

Big Loaf BLT

SERVES 4 TO 6

Most BLTs don't hold up very well and should be enjoyed shortly after they are assembled. If you want a BLT on a picnic, you should pack the ingredients separately and make the sandwiches just before serving them. This portable sandwich is an exception to that rule. Made of an entire loaf of bread, it holds up well for a couple of hours; just be sure to bring along a knife and small cutting board.

10 slices bacon, cut in half crosswise
1-pound loaf San Francisco-style sourdough bread,
    cut in half lengthwise
½ cup mayonnaise, more or less to taste
12 fresh basil leaves
5 ripe slicing tomatoes, cored and cut into ¼-inch-
    thick slices
Kosher salt
Black pepper in a mill
3 cups oak-leaf lettuce or shredded romaine lettuce

Preheat the oven to 325°F. Fry the bacon until crisp and transfer onto a brown paper bag to drain. Toast the bread in the oven

84   The BLT Cookbook

until it is hot all the way through and just beginning to turn golden brown on top. Set the hot bread on a work surface.

Spread the mayonnaise over the cut surfaces of the bread. Arrange the basil leaves on the bottom half of the bread and arrange the tomatoes over them. Season the tomatoes with salt and pepper. Set the bacon on top of the tomatoes, top them with the lettuce, and cover with the top half of the bread. To serve immediately, cut into crosswise sections. To serve later, wrap in aluminum foil and serve within an hour or two.

VARIATION: Omit the basil. Peel 1 or 2 avocados, mash the meat with a fork, season with salt and pepper, and spread over the bread before adding the tomatoes.

Big Loaf BLT Po'Boy with Fried Oysters and Tabasco Hollandaise

SERVES 4 TO 6

The secret to preparing oysters, rather than just eating them raw on the half shell, is to cook them briefly, just long enough for them to shrink, which they do within seconds of hitting a hot pan. In this recipe, hollandaise sauce replaces mayonnaise; it's difficult to make a small quantity of the sauce, so you'll likely have some left over, which you can reheat in a double boiler over lightly simmering water and serve with roasted asparagus.

Tabasco Hollandaise (recipe follows)
2 eggs, beaten
1 cup fresh bread crumbs, from sourdough bread, or
    ½ cup cornmeal
1 pint freshly shucked oysters (see Note)
8 slices bacon, cut in half crosswise
1-pound loaf San Francisco–style sourdough bread,
    cut in half lengthwise
2 to 3 tablespoons clarified butter or bacon fat
5 ripe slicing tomatoes, cored and cut into ¼-inch
    slices
Kosher salt
Black pepper in a mill

3 cups shredded iceberg lettuce, from outer leaves only
1 lemon, cut into wedges

First, make the hollandaise and keep it warm.

Put the eggs in a medium bowl, and put the bread crumbs or cornmeal in a separate medium bowl. Cover a sheet pan with absorbent paper. Dip each oyster in egg, then turn it in the bread crumbs so that it is evenly coated. Set the oysters on the sheet pan.

Preheat the oven to 325°F. Fry the bacon until crisp and drain on a brown paper bag. Toast the bread in the oven until it is hot all the way through and just beginning to turn golden brown on top. Set the hot bread on a work surface.

Melt the clarified butter or bacon fat in a heavy sauté pan set over medium heat. When the butter is foamy or the bacon fat melted and hot, sauté the oysters, working in batches, until they just barely shrink, about 30 seconds on each side. Transfer to the sheet pan.

Arrange the tomatoes on top of the bottom piece of bread and season them with salt and pepper. Set the bacon on top of the tomatoes and arrange the oysters on top of the bacon. Spoon hollandaise over it all, set the lettuce on top, and cap with the top piece of bread. Cut into crosswise sections and serve immediately with lemon wedges on the side.

NOTE: Fresh oysters are available in the meat and seafood departments of better supermarkets or specialty markets. Ask the clerk to shuck them for you. The number required to make a pint will vary greatly depending on the type of oyster; smaller ones are best for this recipe.

VARIATION: Add a generous smear of Rémoulade Sauce (page 134) or Smoky Romesco Sauce (page 136) to the bread before adding the tomatoes. Use either the hollandaise or one of these sauces to top the sandwich.

Tabasco Hollandaise

MAKES ABOUT 1 CUP

> 1 extra large or 2 medium egg yolks
> 1 tablespoon fresh lemon juice
> 1 teaspoon Tabasco sauce
> Kosher salt
> Black pepper in a mill
> 12 tablespoons (1½ sticks) butter, melted and
>   bubbling hot

Prepare a double boiler over very low heat; do not let the water boil.

Put the egg yolks in a medium bowl and whip vigorously with a whisk until they turn pale yellow. Whisk in the lemon juice and Tabasco sauce and season lightly with salt and pepper. Slowly pour in the hot butter, whisking all the while. When all of the butter has been incorporated, taste, correct the seasoning, and keep warm in the double boiler until ready to use.

New York City's Finest BLTs

Chat 'n Chew, 10 East 16th Street, between Fifth Avenue and Union Square West

City Bakery, 22 East 17th Street, between Broadway and Fifth Avenue

Daddy-O, 44 Bedford Street, near Seventh Avenue South

First, 87 First Avenue, between 5th and 6th Streets

Good, 89 Greenwich, near 12th Street

'ino, Bedford Street, between Sixth Avenue and Downing Street

Island Burgers, 766 Ninth Avenue, between 51st and 52nd Streets

Union Square Cafe, 21 East 16th Street, between Fifth Avenue and Union Square West

Side by Side

There's always something beside a BLT, a tasty distraction that allows us to extend our little feast. In truck stops, diners, and cafés, it will be potato chips, shoestring potatoes, fries, onion rings, macaroni salad, coleslaw, potato salad, cottage cheese, or dill pickle wedges. A trendy restaurant in California, New York, or Hawaii may offer taro, sweet potato, or beet chips, a mix of all three, or a green salad to balance all that bacon. I like pickled onions, bread-and-butter pickles, or skin-on fries dipped in homemade mayonnaise. A segment on the popular public radio program "This American Life" tells the story of a student posing as a vegetarian who sneaks away to enjoy an illicit meal: a BLT and fries with meat gravy, a New England specialty.

Salads Inspired by the BLT

Tomato Salad with Bacon Vinaigrette

When you want the flavors and textures of a BLT in a refined context, try this seductive salad.

For the Vinaigrette
6 slices bacon
3 shallots, minced
2 garlic cloves, minced
½ cup red wine vinegar, 6 percent acidity, plus more
    as needed
Kosher salt
Black pepper in a mill
½ cup olive oil, plus more as needed
3 tablespoons minced fresh flat-leaf parsley

For the Salad
8 cups small oak-leaf lettuce leaves
10 to 12 small slicing tomatoes of various colors
6 to 8 slices country-style bread
½ cup *fromage blanc* or fresh ricotta
¼ cup extra virgin olive oil
Kosher salt
Black pepper in a mill
¼ cup Toasted Bread Crumbs (page 138)

First, make the vinaigrette. Fry the bacon in a medium sauté pan until almost crisp; transfer onto a brown paper bag to drain. Add the shallots to the bacon fat and sauté until soft, 6 to 7 minutes; add the garlic and sauté 2 minutes more. Add the vinegar, simmer until it is reduced by half, season with salt and pepper, stir in the olive oil, and remove from the heat. Stir the mixture, taste, and correct the acid-oil balance if necessary. Correct the seasoning, stir in the parsley, and set aside. Mince the bacon and set it aside.

Spread the lettuce over a large platter.

Remove the core of each tomato and cut it into six wedges. Put the cut tomatoes into a large mixing bowl and pour about half of the vinaigrette over them; toss gently.

Toast the bread until it is golden brown. Spread a little *fromage blanc* or ricotta over the bread, drizzle with olive oil, and season with salt and pepper.

Spoon the tomatoes and any juices that have collected in the bowl over the lettuce. Heat the remaining vinaigrette, add the minced bacon, pour it over the tomatoes and greens, and scatter the bread crumbs on top. Arrange the toast around the edge of the platter and serve immediately.

Bread Salad with Bacon, Tomatoes, Onions, and Olives

All cooks should have a bread salad in their repertoire. They are easy to make, delicious, and a great use for bread that is too stale for sandwiches.

6 slices bacon

⅔ cup extra virgin olive oil

2 tablespoons red wine vinegar, 6 percent acidity

Juice of 1 lemon

2 garlic cloves, minced

Kosher salt

Black pepper in a mill

4 cups stale Italian bread, cut into 1-inch cubes

2 cups cherry tomatoes, halved

1 small red onion, diced

3 tablespoons minced fresh flat-leaf parsley

½ cup pitted Kalamata olives, sliced

1 quart fresh salad greens

In a heavy skillet, fry the bacon until it is just crisp. Transfer the bacon onto a brown paper bag to drain. Pour the bacon drippings into a small mixing bowl and whisk in the olive oil. Add the vinegar, lemon juice, and garlic. Season with salt and pepper, taste, and add more vinegar if needed for balance. In a large mixing bowl, toss together the bread and all but 3 tablespoons of the dressing. Let sit for 30 minutes.

To serve, toss the bread with the tomatoes, onion, parsley, and olives. Spread the salad greens over a serving platter, put the bread salad on top, and drizzle the remaining dressing over all. Crumble the bacon on top and serve immediately.

Pasta Salad with Bacon, Tomatoes, and Bocconcini

SERVES 6 TO 8

There are two essential rules when making pasta salad. First, it must be served at room temperature, not cold. Second, it should be dressed lightly, more like a green salad than a potato salad.

> 1 tablespoon kosher salt, plus more to taste
> 8 ounces *orecchiette*, dried gnocchi, or medium
>   shells
> 6 slices bacon
> ⅓ cup extra virgin olive oil
> 3 cups cherry tomatoes, halved or quartered
> 6 ounces *bocconcini*, halved
> 4 cups shredded romaine lettuce
> 2 cups toasted croutons (see Note)
> Black pepper in a mill
> ⅓ cup mayonnaise, thinned with a little warm
>   water or lemon juice, in a squeeze bottle

Fill a medium pot two-thirds full with water, add the tablespoon of kosher salt, and bring to a boil over high heat. Add the pasta, stir, and cook until al dente; taste during the last minute or so to determine exactly when the pasta is done. Drain the pasta,

rinse it thoroughly in cool water, and put it in a wide serving bowl.

While the pasta cooks, fry the bacon in a medium sauté pan until it is crisp. Transfer onto brown paper bag to drain and then crumble.

Pour the olive oil over the pasta, add the cherry tomatoes and cheese, and toss gently. Add the shredded lettuce and the croutons, season with black pepper, and toss again. Drizzle the mayonnaise over the salad, scatter the bacon on top, and serve immediately.

NOTE: To make croutons, cut country-style bread into ¾-inch cubes and put the cubes into a widemouth quart jar. Add 2 tablespoons of olive oil, secure the jar's lid, and shake gently until the olive oil is evenly distributed. Season with salt and pepper and shake again. Spread the croutons over a baking sheet and toast in a 300°F oven until golden brown, 15 to 20 minutes.

Composed Salad with Spaghettini, Smoked Mozzarella, Tomatoes, and Bacon

SERVES 6 TO 8

If you use small plum tomatoes, you don't need to peel them. If you use larger tomatoes, peel them before you slice them into wedges.

1 tablespoon kosher salt, plus more to taste
8 ounces spaghettini
½ cup extra virgin olive oil
8 thick slices bacon, cut crosswise into ⅜-inch strips
1 small head romaine lettuce, shredded
8 ounces *mozzarella di bufalo affumicata,* or other
   smoked fresh mozzarella, shredded
12 to 15 small plum tomatoes, cut lengthwise into
   wedges
2 tablespoons minced fresh basil
2 tablespoons minced fresh parsley
2 tablespoons minced fresh oregano
1 cup toasted croutons (see page 97)

Fill a large pot two-thirds full with water, add the tablespoon of kosher salt, and bring to a boil over high heat. Add the pasta, stir, and cook until al dente; check the package for the exact cooking time and taste during the last minute or so to determine exactly when the pasta is done. Drain the pasta, rinse it in cool water, and put it in a mixing bowl. Drizzle a tablespoon or so of the olive oil over the pasta and toss thoroughly.

Meanwhile, fry the bacon until it is just crisp; transfer it onto a brown paper bag to drain.

Put the lettuce in a deep, clear glass salad bowl, sprinkle a little salt over it, and toss gently. Add the pasta, spreading it out in an even layer over the lettuce. Top the pasta with the cheese and spread the bacon over the cheese. In a small bowl, season the tomatoes with salt and pepper and spread them on top of the salad. Mix together the remaining olive oil and the herbs and pour the mixture over the tomatoes. Cover and let rest at room temperature for 15 minutes before serving.

To serve, scatter the croutons on top, toss the salad at the table, and use tongs to serve it.

Potato Salad with Bacon and Tomatoes

One of the best potato salads I've tasted was made by my friend Mary Duryee and serves as inspiration here. The cherry tomatoes were perfectly ripe, cucumbers offered a refreshing touch, the dressing was both tart and rich. When I asked how she made it, she said, "I have no idea, I just made it."

2½ pounds small new potatoes, scrubbed
Kosher salt
8 slices bacon
1 yellow onion, minced
1 cucumber, preferably Armenian, cut into half
    moons
4 scallions, trimmed, and cut into thin rounds
Black pepper in a mill
¼ cup olive oil
3 tablespoons red wine vinegar
3 tablespoons minced fresh flat-leaf parsley
3 cups cherry tomatoes, halved

Cut the potatoes into thin slices, put them in a large saucepan, cover with water plus 2 inches, and add a tablespoon of kosher salt. Bring to a boil over high heat, reduce the heat to medium low, and simmer until the potatoes are tender, 12 to 18 minutes. Drain thoroughly and put the potatoes into a wide bowl.

Meanwhile, cook the bacon until it is crisp and transfer it onto a brown paper bag to drain. Pour the bacon fat over the hot cooked potatoes and toss gently. Add the onion, cucumber, and scallions, season with black pepper, and let rest for about 15 minutes, until the potatoes are nearly at room temperature. Crumble the bacon.

In a small bowl, combine the olive oil, red wine vinegar, and parsley. Taste, season with salt and pepper, and balance with more oil, if necessary. Pour the dressing over the salad. Quickly fold in the tomatoes and half of the bacon, taste, and correct the seasoning. Scatter the remaining bacon over the top of the salad and serve within 30 minutes.

Pasta, Rice, Pudding, and Pie

Creamy Pasta with Tomatoes, Pancetta, and Fresh Herbs

SERVES 4 TO 6

"So, this is for the BLT book, right?" my daughter Gina said as I served her a version of this recipe. It hadn't occurred to me, but I saw her point; there is something about the melting *fromage blanc* and the pancetta that evokes our favorite sandwich. Adding tomatoes makes the resonance even stronger.

Kosher salt

1 pound dried gnocchi

3 tablespoons olive oil

2 medium shallots

3 to 4 ounces pancetta, diced

6 garlic cloves

3 cups cherry tomatoes, halved or quartered

6 ounces *fromage blanc*

2 tablespoons minced fresh flat-leaf parsley

1 tablespoon fresh snipped chives

1 teaspoon minced fresh oregano

1 teaspoon minced fresh thyme

Black pepper in a mill

3 tablespoons best-quality extra virgin
    olive oil

⅓ cup Toasted Bread Crumbs (page 138)

Fill a medium pot two-thirds full with water, add a tablespoon of kosher salt, and bring to a boil over high heat. Add the pasta, stir, and cook until al dente; taste during the last minute or so to determine exactly when the pasta is done. Drain but do not rinse the pasta, and put it in a low, wide bowl. Cover with a tea towel to keep warm.

Meanwhile, heat the olive oil in a sauté pan set over medium-low heat, add the shallots, and sauté until soft, about 5 minutes. Add the pancetta and continue to cook, stirring now and then, until the pancetta is nearly crisp. Add the garlic and sauté 2 minutes more. Increase the heat to high, add the tomatoes, and sauté, tossing constantly, for 30 seconds.

Add the *fromage blanc*, herbs, and cherry tomato mixture to the pasta and toss gently but thoroughly. Drizzle the olive oil on top, toss again, and sprinkle with the bread crumbs. Serve immediately.

Pappardelle, Bacon, and Zucchini with Warm Tomato Vinaigrette

SERVES 4 TO 6

Pappardelle is a broad noodle, usually about 1¼ inches wide. It offers a wonderful sensation on the palate that is both tender and voluptuous.

> 2 small shallots, minced
> 4 tablespoons sherry vinegar
> 2 cups Tomato Concassé (page 132)
> Kosher salt
> Black pepper in a mill
> ⅔ cup extra virgin olive oil, plus more for the
>   zucchini
> 3 tablespoons minced fresh flat-leaf parsley
> 3 medium zucchini, 5 to 6 inches long, cut
>   lengthwise into very thin strips
> 8 ounces pappardelle
> 4 to 6 slices bacon, cut in half lengthwise

Put the shallots in a medium bowl, pour the vinegar over them, and set aside for 15 or 20 minutes. Stir in the tomato concassé, season with salt and pepper, and stir in the olive oil and two tablespoons of the parsley. Taste, correct the seasoning, and set aside.

Fill a large pot two-thirds full with water, add a tablespoon of kosher salt, and bring to a boil over high heat. Add the pasta, stir, and cook until al dente; check the package for the exact cooking time and taste during the last minute or so to determine exactly when the pasta is done. (If you are using fresh rather than dried pasta, do not cook it until the bacon is fried.)

Meanwhile, set a ridged frying pan or a sauté pan over medium heat, brush the zucchini strips with a little olive oil, and fry them, turning once, for 6 to 8 minutes, until they are tender. Remove from the heat and keep warm.

Fry the bacon until it is just barely crisp. Drain it on a brown paper bag.

When the pasta is tender, drain it and put it into a wide serving bowl. Add the zucchini strips, bacon, and half the tomato vinaigrette, and toss together very gently. Spoon the remaining vinaigrette over the mixture, sprinkle the remaining parsley on top, and serve immediately.

Pasta with Tomato Wedges, Bacon, and Shredded Romaine

Cream plays as crucial a role in this dish as mayonnaise does on a BLT. Here, it picks up the smoky, salty flavors of the bacon and the acidity of the tomatoes, distributing them to the other ingredients to create a bowl-lickin'-good pasta.

> 1 tablespoon kosher salt
> 1 pound dried spaghetti
> 6 thick slices bacon, cut crosswise into ⅜-inch-wide
>   strips
> 2 tablespoons olive oil
> 8 small to medium slicing tomatoes, cored and cut
>   into wedges
> Kosher salt
> Black pepper in a mill
> ½ cup heavy cream
> 8 to 10 medium romaine lettuce leaves, cut
>   crosswise into ¼-inch-wide strips

Fill a medium pot two-thirds full with water, add the tablespoon of kosher salt, and bring to a boil over high heat. Add the pasta, stir, and cook until al dente; taste during the last minute or so to determine exactly when the pasta is done. Drain but do not rinse the pasta and put it in a low, wide bowl. Cover with a tea towel to keep warm.

Meanwhile, cook the bacon in a medium sauté pan until it is almost crisp. Transfer it onto a brown paper bag to drain. Pour off all but 2 tablespoons of bacon fat from the pan, add the olive oil, and return the pan to medium heat. Add half the tomatoes and sauté them for 1 minute. Season with salt and pepper, turn, sauté for 1 minute more, and season again with salt and pepper. Transfer the tomatoes to the bowl with the pasta, return the pan to the heat, and cook the remaining tomatoes, seasoning them on both sides with salt and pepper. Transfer them to the bowl.

Pour the heavy cream into the pan and swirl to pick up all of the pan juices. When the cream just begins to simmer, pour it over the pasta. Toss the pasta and tomatoes gently but thoroughly.

Add the sliced lettuce to the pasta, toss gently, scatter the bacon on top, and serve immediately.

Risotto with Bacon,
Lettuce, and Tomato Concassé

Excellent bacon is essential in this risotto. A small amount of its fat infuses the rice with a wonderfully smoky flavor.

1½ cups Tomato Concassé (page 132)
4 to 6 thick slices bacon
1 tablespoon butter
1 small yellow onion, diced
2 garlic cloves, minced
Kosher salt
Black pepper in a mill
5 to 6 cups homemade Chicken Broth (page 140)
1¼ cups Vialone Nano or Carnaroli rice
3 ounces dry Jack or aged Asiago, grated (about
    ¾ cup)
3 tablespoons minced fresh flat-leaf parsley
10 romaine lettuce leaves, each 4 to 5 inches long,
    cut into chiffonade (see page 124)

Make the tomato concassé and set it aside.

Fry the bacon in a deep saucepan, such as a 12-inch saucier, until it is almost crisp. Transfer the bacon onto a brown paper bag to

drain; crumble or mince the bacon and cover to keep it warm. Pour off all but 1 tablespoon of the fat from the pan, reduce the heat to low, add the butter, and when it melts, add the onion. Sauté until the onion is soft, 8 to 10 minutes. Add the garlic and sauté for 2 minutes more. Season with salt and pepper.

Meanwhile, pour the chicken broth into a saucepan, bring to a boil, and reduce the heat so that the broth simmers.

Add the rice to the onions and garlic and stir with a wooden spoon until each grain turns milky white, about 2 minutes. Add broth ½ cup at a time, stirring after each addition until the liquid is absorbed.

Continue adding broth and stirring until the rice is tender, 20 to 22 minutes total cooking time. When the rice is tender, stir in the cheese and parsley, and correct the seasoning. Stir in a final ¼ cup of broth.

Quickly divide the tomato concassé among warmed individual soup plates, agitating each plate so that the concassé spreads over its surface. Divide the risotto among the plates, spooning it on top of the tomatoes. Sprinkle bacon and scatter lettuce over each portion and serve immediately.

Tomatoes Stuffed with Bacon Risotto

The first summer tomatoes are too precious to bake, but by fall, when they must be enjoyed, preserved, or lost, baking them is a great way to savor them, especially on a cool evening.

6 medium slicing tomatoes
2 to 2½ cups Risotto with Bacon (page 110)
Olive oil
6 cups fresh red-leaf lettuce
Kosher salt
Black pepper in a mill
3 tablespoons minced fresh flat-leaf parsley

Preheat the oven to 325°F.

Cut off the top (stem end) of each tomato by making a crosswise slice just above the shoulder. Use a teaspoon to scoop out all the flesh, gel, and seeds of the tomato, leaving only the skin and the layer of flesh attached to it.

Fill each tomato with risotto and set the filled tomatoes into a baking dish that has been brushed with olive oil. Bake until the risotto is hot and the tomatoes tender, 20 to 25 minutes.

Put the lettuce in a medium mixing bowl, sprinkle a little salt over it, and toss gently. Add a tablespoon or two of olive oil, toss again, season with black pepper and toss again. Divide the lettuce among individual plates and set a tomato on top of each portion. Sprinkle parsley on top of the risotto and serve immediately.

NOTE: You can use any leftover risotto to make this dish, or you can make it fresh. The exact quantity you need will vary, depending on the size of your tomatoes.

Tomato Bread Pudding

The brioche, a slightly sweet bread made with eggs, milk, and butter, nearly vanishes into this pudding, creating a pillowy, hedonistic tenderness. Serve as a first course or as a side dish with roasted chicken or grilled meat or seafood.

Olive oil

8 ounces dry-cured bacon

6 cups brioche, torn into medium chunks

1 cup Tomato Concassé (page 132)

3 tablespoons finely minced fresh flat-leaf
    parsley

2 ounces Gruyère, Fontina, or St. George cheese,
    grated (about ½ cups)

1 whole egg

2 egg yolks

2½ cups milk

2 tablespoons puréed sun-dried tomatoes

2 cloves garlic, finely minced or pressed

Kosher salt

Black pepper in a mill

1 quart fresh salad greens, lightly salted

Rub a 2-quart baking dish with olive oil. Fry the bacon until it is almost crisp and transfer it onto a brown paper bag to drain. Put the brioche chunks in a large mixing bowl. Let the pan drippings cool briefly, and then pour them over the bread, tossing thoroughly. Add the tomato concassé, parsley, and cheese and toss again. Crumble the bacon, add it to the mixture, and toss lightly. Transfer the mixture to the baking dish.

Whisk together the whole egg, egg yolks, milk, tomato purée, and garlic. Season with a generous pinch of salt and several turns of black pepper. Pour the custard over the bread and agitate the dish so that the liquid is distributed evenly. Bake in a 325°F oven for 35 minutes. Increase the heat to 425°F and bake for an additional 10 to 15 minutes, until the top of the pudding is lightly and evenly browned. Let rest at least 10 minutes before serving alongside the salad greens.

Bacon, Leek, and Tomato Strudel

Here, mildly tangy dough replaces the bread of a BLT, while the cheese contributes a rich element usually added by mayonnaise. Serve for brunch or lunch on a weekend, when guests can linger around the table and enjoy a glass or two of chilled dry rosé, the perfect accompaniment.

For the Dough
1 cup (2 sticks) unsalted butter, at room
    temperature
1 cup cream cheese, preferably old-fashioned, at
    room temperature
2½ cups all-purpose flour
1 teaspoon kosher salt
½ cup heavy cream

For the Filling
6 slices bacon
1 tablespoon butter
2 medium leeks, white and pale green part only,
    very thinly sliced and thoroughly rinsed
Kosher salt
Black pepper in a mill
3 to 4 medium tomatoes, such as Black Brandywine

6 ounces *Doux de Montagne,* Italian Fontina, or
Emmentaler, thinly sliced
3 tablespoons fresh snipped chives
1 teaspoon Hawaiian alaea salt, optional
1 tablespoon white sesame seeds, lightly toasted
1 egg white, mixed with 1 tablespoon water
6 cups fresh salad greens

To make the dough, use an electric mixer or wooden spoon to combine the butter and cream cheese in a large mixing bowl. When it is smooth and creamy, sift the flour and salt together, and gradually add the mixture to the cheese and butter. Stir in the cream, cover, and refrigerate for 1 hour.

To make the filling, fry the bacon in a medium sauté pan until it is just crisp. Transfer it onto a brown paper bag and, when it has drained, crumble it. Drain off all but 1 tablespoon of the bacon fat from the pan, return the pan to the heat, add the butter, and when it is melted, add the leeks. Cook the leeks, stirring occasionally, until they are very tender, 10 to 12 minutes. Season with salt and pepper and remove from the heat.

Remove the stem core of each tomato, cut the tomatoes into 3/8-inch-thick slices, set on a platter, sprinkle with kosher salt, and set aside, covered. (If the tomatoes are particularly large, cut the slices in half before salting.)

Preheat the oven to 400°F and prepare a baking sheet, oiling it lightly or using a nonstick mat.

To assemble the strudel, dust a work surface with flour and roll out the dough to form a 10-inch by 14-inch rectangle. Arrange the cheese lengthwise down the center of the dough and spoon the leeks on top of it. Drain off any juices that have collected on the tomatoes and arrange the slices over the cheese and leeks. Sprinkle the chives and the bacon on top.

Fold the edges of the pastry over to form a long cylinder, brush the inner edges with egg white, and press with a fork to seal tightly.

Use a mortar and pestle or *suribachi* (a ridged Japanese mortar) to grind the alaea salt and toasted sesame seeds together until most of the seeds are broken. Brush the top of the pastry with the remaining egg white and sprinkle the sesame seed mixture on top. Use a sharp knife to make crosswise slashes every 2 inches in the pastry. Do not cut too deeply.

Transfer the strudel to the baking sheet and bake for 25 minutes, or until the pastry is golden brown. Remove from the oven, let rest 10 minutes, cut into wedges, using the slashes as a guide, and serve immediately with salad greens on the side.

Fresh Tomato Pie with Bacon and Mayonnaise

SERVES 6 TO 8

You shouldn't let summer pass without making this luscious pie at least once. With a simple green salad alongside, your meal will have all the elements of a BLT.

For the Crust

2 cups all-purpose flour

2 teaspoons black peppercorns, crushed fine

Kosher salt

1 tablespoon baking powder

8 tablespoons (1 stick) butter, cut into small cubes
    and chilled

⅔ cup whole milk

For the Filling

8 slices bacon

3 pounds medium ripe tomatoes, peeled (page 132)

¼ cup minced fresh flat-leaf parsley

2 tablespoons minced fresh basil

2 tablespoons fresh snipped chives

6 ounces medium-sharp Cheddar, grated
    (about 1½ cups)

⅔ cup mayonnaise

Juice of 1 lemon

2 tablespoons heavy cream

In a medium bowl, combine the flour, pepper, 1 teaspoon kosher salt, and the baking powder. Use a pastry blender to quickly work the butter into the flour mixture until it is fully incorporated and has an evenly grainy texture. Make a small well in the center of the flour, pour the milk in, and mix quickly with a fork until the dough comes together but remains soft and sticky.

Turn the dough onto a floured surface, knead for 30 seconds, and then cover with a tea towel. Let the dough rest for 10 minutes.

Meanwhile, remove the stem cores of the tomatoes and cut them into ⅜-inch-thick slices. Set the tomatoes in a large colander set over a bowl, sprinkle with a teaspoon or two of kosher salt, and toss very gently. Let the tomatoes drain for about 20 minutes; toss them gently now and then as they drain.

Preheat the oven to 375°F. Cut the rested dough in half, roll one piece into a 12-inch circle, and line a 10-inch glass or ceramic pie pan with it.

In a small bowl, toss together the parsley, basil, and chives. Put a layer of tomato slices on top of the pastry dough, season with a little salt and pepper, sprinkle with some of the herbs, and repeat with a second layer of tomatoes. Season with salt and pepper, and scatter some of the bacon on top. Repeat with a third layer of tomatoes and herbs and a fourth layer of tomatoes and bacon. Scatter the cheese on top.

Thin the mayonnaise with the lemon juice and carefully spread it over the top of the pie. Quickly roll out the reserved dough, fit it over the pie, and seal the edges by pinching them together.

Make several cuts in the top of the pie to allow steam to escape, and brush the surface of the dough with the cream.

Bake until the pie is steaming hot and the crust is golden brown, 35 to 40 minutes. Let rest for 15 minutes before serving.

Basic Recipes

To Shred Lettuce and Large-leafed Herbs

A flurry of thinly shredded herbs or greens is called a *chiffonade*. To make it, stack several leaves and hold them on your work surface with one hand. Using a very sharp knife, cut thin ribbons. After all of the greens have been thusly shredded, fluff with your fingers and use as directed.

Mayonnaise, with
Nine Variations

Mayonnaise is the classic cold emulsion, a mother recipe upon which many sauces are built. Its history dates back hundreds of years. It could have not have survived through countless historical and environmental upheavals if it were difficult to make. The formula is simple: a large quantity of oil is suspended in a small quantity of liquid, with the lecithin in egg yolk serving as the emulsifier that keeps the mixture stable. If you add oil slowly, you will make a successful sauce. The flavor depends upon the ingredients themselves. Use excellent eggs from a local farmer, and a mild olive oil, such as a late-harvest oil from either California or Liguria in northern Italy. Late-harvest oils are sweeter and less bitter than others. Some chefs recommend neutral oil such as canola or grape seed, but I prefer extra virgin olive oil because it is more environmentally friendly. Hexene is used to extract canola, grape seed, and refined olive oils and is released into the atmosphere after production. Extra virgin olive oil is extracted mechanically, not chemically.

This recipe can easily be doubled, and a double batch can be made in a food processor; this single-egg-yolk version must be made by hand.

1 large egg yolk
Generous pinch kosher salt, plus more as needed

Black pepper in a mill
1 teaspoon fresh lemon juice, plus more to taste
1 cup extra virgin olive oil, preferably a late-harvest
variety
1 tablespoon boiling water

Put the egg yolk in a small glass, stainless steel, or ceramic mixing bowl. Whisk in the salt, several turns of black pepper, and the lemon juice. Slowly begin to whisk in the oil, a drop or two at a time. As the emulsion forms, you can add the oil slightly more quickly. Continue whisking as the sauce thickens and increases in volume. When all of the oil has been incorporated, taste the mayonnaise. If it needs more salt, dissolve a generous pinch in the boiling water and whisk the water into the mayonnaise. If you prefer more tartness, whisk in a squeeze of lemon juice before adding the boiling water.

Cover the mayonnaise with plastic wrap and refrigerate for at least 1 hour before using. Properly chilled, the sauce will keep for 2 to 3 days.

BALSAMIC MAYONNAISE   Omit the lemon juice. Use ½ to 1 teaspoon *aceto balsamico tradizionale* and a pinch of sugar.

CAPER MAYONNAISE   Add 2 tablespoons minced drained capers and 1 mashed anchovy.

CAVIAR MAYONNAISE   Add 1 tablespoon sevruga caviar just before using the mayonnaise.

CHIPOTLE MAYONNAISE   Omit the lemon juice; dissolve $\frac{1}{8}$ teaspoon chipotle powder in 1 teaspoon lime juice before adding it to the egg.

DRIED-TOMATO MAYONNAISE   Add 2 tablespoons puréed dried tomatoes.

HERB MAYONNAISE   Add 2 tablespoons fresh herbs of choice before chilling the mayonnaise. Use fines herbes (equal amounts of chives, chervil, parsley, and tarragon) in the spring; use basil alone in the summer.

LEMON ZEST MAYONNAISE   Add 2 teaspoons finely grated lemon zest before chilling the mayonnaise.

LIME-JALAPEÑO MAYONNAISE   Use lime juice instead of lemon juice. Add half a minced jalapeño chile and 2 tablespoons minced cilantro leaves before chilling the mayonnaise.

OLIVE MAYONNAISE   Add 2 tablespoons olive tapenade.

Aïoli, by Hand

True aïoli packs a powerful punch, an intensity that overwhelms many American palates. If you are not used to a bold aïoli, begin with two or three garlic cloves and gradually increase the number as your tolerance and enjoyment increase. Then you can add even more cloves if you like; just be sure to let the sauce rest a while before serving it, so that the flavors are in balance.

2 to 10 large garlic cloves, crushed
Kosher salt
1 large egg yolk
¾ to 1 cup extra virgin olive oil
White pepper in a mill
1 to 2 teaspoons fresh lemon juice, optional
1 tablespoon boiling water

Put the crushed garlic into a *suribachi* (Japanese mortar), add a generous pinch of salt, and grind it with a wooden pestle until it is reduced to a liquidy pulp. Add the egg yolk and mix it with the garlic until a thick paste is formed. Begin adding oil, a bit at a time, mixing all the while. Continue until the mixture is thick and resists absorbing more oil. Season with several turns of white pepper. Taste the aïoli and if it is bitter, or if it needs salt, squeeze about 2 teaspoons of lemon juice on top, add about ½ teaspoon salt, and swirl the juice to dissolve the salt. Mix gently. Whisk in the boiling water, cover the sauce, and refrigerate for 1 hour before serving. Aïoli will keep, covered, in the refrigerator for 2 to 3 days.

Aïoli, by Machine

Aïoli made in a food processor is not as voluptuous as that made by hand, but there are times when it is the best technique. In very hot weather, handmade aïoli can break; machine-made aïoli is more stable and will remain emulsified even when temperatures soar. You cannot, however, make a small quantity. To make aïoli using just one egg yolk, you must use a mortar and pestle or a *suribachi*.

> 1 garlic bulb, cloves separated and peeled, or more
>   or less to taste
> 1 whole egg
> 2 egg yolks
> 1 teaspoon kosher salt, plus more to taste
> 2 cups mild extra virgin olive oil
> 1 to 2 tablespoons fresh lemon juice, optional

Put the garlic cloves, whole egg, egg yolks, and salt in the work bowl of a food processor and pulse for about 45 seconds, until the garlic is nearly completely puréed. With the machine running, slowly drizzle in the olive oil, using the tube provided, or carefully drizzling by hand. When all of the oil is incorporated, taste the sauce. If it seems a little bland or unfocused, dissolve about ½ teaspoon kosher salt in 2 teaspoons of the lemon juice. With the machine running, pour the mixture into the aïoli. Taste again, and repeat with more lemon juice and a pinch of salt until the sauce comes together. Transfer the aïoli to a bowl and, if it is too stiff, whisk in a tablespoon of boiling water. Cover and let rest in the refrigerator for at least 30 minutes before serving.

Tomato Concassé

Tomato concassé scares some home cooks, probably because its name makes it sound more complex than it actually is. Nothing more than fresh tomatoes reduced to a pulp and seasoned with salt, it is a building block for many recipes. It is not always drained as it is here, but for the recipes in this book it is best to do so. Save the flavorful liquid that drains to use in other recipes, such as Butter Lettuce Soup (page 40).

2 pounds medium or large vine-ripened tomatoes
Kosher salt

First, peel the tomatoes. To do so, turn a burner on a gas or electric stove to high. Spear a tomato through its stem end on the tines of a dinner (not salad) fork. Hold the tomato close to the heat, turning it quickly as the skin shrinks, cracks, and blisters; this will take between 10 and 20 seconds. Set the tomato on a baking sheet or in a wide bowl to cool and continue until all of the tomatoes have been similarly seared.

Beginning with the first tomato, which will by now be cool enough to handle, use your fingers to pull off and discard the skin. Use a paring knife to cut out the stem cores, and cut each tomato in half crosswise through the tomato's equator.

Next, remove the seeds and gel. Hold one tomato half, cut side down, over a bowl and gently squeeze. The seeds and gel should drop out easily; if they don't, use a finger to coax them out.

When all of the tomatoes have been seared, peeled, and seeded, set them on a wooden cutting board. Set a medium strainer over a large bowl.

Chop the tomatoes into small pieces, until they are nearly reduced to a pulp. Transfer the pulp to the strainer and let them drain for 5 minutes; stir the tomatoes now and then as they drain.

Transfer the drained pulp, or concassé, to a glass bowl, season to taste with salt, and set aside until ready to use. Store the juice that remains in the bowl to use in another recipe.

Rémoulade Sauce

I am so used to enjoying this sauce on shellfish that I practically taste the crab itself in the dressing, which is similar to Russian Dressing, popular in the 1950s over a wedge of iceberg lettuce.

1 cup mayonnaise, preferably homemade
⅓ cup ketchup
2 tablespoons Dijon mustard
1 tablespoon prepared horseradish
3 tablespoons snipped fresh chives
2 tablespoons minced fresh flat-leaf parsley
2 tablespoons minced preserved lemon
Several shakes Worcestershire sauce
Several shakes Tabasco sauce
Black pepper in a mill
Kosher salt, if needed

Combine the mayonnaise, ketchup, mustard, and horseradish in a medium bowl. Fold in the chives, parsley, and preserved lemon. Add the Worcestershire sauce, Tabasco sauce, and several turns of black pepper. Mix thoroughly, taste, and correct the balance of flavors: if the sauce is too tart, add a bit more mayonnaise; if it is not sweet enough, add a bit more ketchup. If it tastes flat, dissolve a generous pinch of kosher salt in a teaspoon of warm water and stir it into the sauce. Use immediately, or cover and refrigerate for up to a week.

Smoky Romesco Sauce

The smoky chipotle in this sauce resonates with the bacon in any of the recipes in this book. For vegetarians, it can provide some of the smoky flavor that is missing when the bacon is omitted.

> 1 chipotle chile
> 2 egg yolks
> 5 garlic cloves
> ¼ cup slivered almonds, toasted
> 1 red bell pepper, roasted, peeled, seeded
>   (see Note), and chopped
> 1 small (2-inch) tomato, peeled and seeded
> 1¼ cups extra virgin olive oil
> Kosher salt
> Black pepper in a mill
> ¼ cup red wine vinegar
> 2 tablespoons fresh lemon juice

At least 30 minutes before making the sauce, put the chipotle chile in a small bowl and pour ½ cup boiling water over it. Set it aside.

Drain and dry the chile, remove its stem, and put it in a food processor, along with the egg yolks, garlic, and almonds, and pulse until the mixture is reduced to a smooth paste. Add the pepper and tomato, pulse several times, and slowly drizzle in half the olive oil, operating the machine continuously. Scrape the sides of the work bowl, season with salt and pepper, and, with the machine operating, add the rest of the olive oil. When all of the oil has been incorporated, add the vinegar and the lemon juice and pulse until smooth. Transfer to a bowl, taste, and correct the seasoning. Cover and chill for 1 hour before using. Properly refrigerated, the sauce will keep for about a week.

NOTE: You can, of course, roast peppers over an open flame, put them in a paper bag to steam for twenty minutes or so, and peel off the charred skin. This works particularly well with thick-skinned peppers. For a more gentle method, use the French technique. Cut off the stem end, remove the seed core, and cut the pepper in half lengthwise. Brush a baking sheet lightly with olive oil, set the pepper halves, cut sides down, on the sheet, brush their skins with a little olive oil, and roast in a 400°F oven for 25 minutes, or until the skin blisters. Cool to room temperature and use your fingers to peel off the skin.

Toasted Bread Crumbs

MAKES 3 CUPS

In my pantry I keep a brown lunch bag in which to save pieces of bread that have gone stale but are still perfect for bread crumbs.

3 cups homemade bread crumbs (see Note)
2 tablespoons olive oil or melted bacon fat

Preheat the oven to 275°F. Put the bread crumbs in a medium bowl, drizzle the olive oil or bacon fat over them and toss gently with your fingers or a fork. Spread the bread crumbs evenly over a rimmed baking sheet, set in the oven, and bake until golden brown, 10 to 12 minutes. Stir once or twice as the bread crumbs toast.

Remove from the oven and use immediately or cool and store in an airtight container.

NOTE: You can make bread crumbs with fresh bread, day-old bread, or bread that is several weeks old, as long as it has been stored properly. To use fresh bread, cut it into cubes, spread the cubes over a baking sheet, and dry in a 250°F oven for 45 minutes. Cool and process, in batches, in a food processor fitted with a metal blade. Day-old or two-day-old bread may not need to be dried in the oven, though if it is too moist it should be. Old bread that is very hard can be grated on the large blades of a box grater.

VARIATION: You can toast bread crumbs on top of the stove, in a wide, heavy skillet set over medium heat. Stir and agitate the pan continuously as the crumbs brown.

Chicken Broth

The difference between chicken broth and chicken stock is in the ratio of meat to bones. Broth has more meat, stock more bones and hence, more gelatin and more structure. When you make broth, the chicken can be eaten; stock is cooked until all of the flavor is extracted and the meat must be discarded. For strong chicken stock, see the variation at the end of this recipe.

> 1 whole chicken, about 4½ pounds, or 4½ pounds
>   leg and thigh pieces
> ⅔ cup kosher salt, plus more for seasoning
> 1 onion, quartered
> 4 garlic cloves, smashed
> 10 flat-leaf parsley sprigs
> 2 teaspoons black peppercorns

Rinse the chicken under cool tap water; pat dry with a tea towel. Fill a large pot two-thirds full with water, add the ⅔ cup kosher salt, and stir until it is dissolved. Plunge the chicken into the brine and let rest for 45 minutes. Drain thoroughly. Put the brined chicken in a large soup pot, cover with 3 quarts (12 cups) of water, and add the onion, cloves, parsley, and peppercorns. Bring to a boil over high heat. When the water boils, reduce the heat to medium low, and simmer very gently, partially covered, until the chicken is completely tender and ready to fall off the bone, about 1½ hours. Remove from the heat and let the chicken sit in the broth as it cools.

Carefully remove the chicken from the pot. Strain the broth into a clean container and discard the vegetables and aromatics. Cool the broth completely and refrigerate for several hours or overnight. Before using, remove the fat that collects on top of the broth.

The chicken broth can be kept in the refrigerator for 4 to 5 days, or frozen for up to 3 months.

STRONG CHICKEN BROTH: After straining the broth, pour it into a clean saucepan and bring it to a boil over medium heat. Simmer the broth until it is reduced by one-half. Cool, refrigerate, and remove the fat before using. Makes 1 quart.

Bacon, at Home

The reason to make bacon at home is because you can and because it's satisfying, just as making your own sauerkraut, preserved lemons, vinegar, or any other staple brings with it a satisfaction that cannot be duplicated by buying even the best product. Plus, if you're a girl, it's a conversation stopper. Announce that you're making your own bacon, and guys look at you with new respect and interest. Now that Niman Ranch sells fresh pork belly through its website (www.nimanranch.com), homemade bacon is within the reach of anyone with time and inclination. You'll also need a smoker. The Little Chief electric smoker is inexpensive and easy to use. I use an inexpensive Brinkman charcoal smoker.

> 1 fresh pork belly, about 6 pounds, skinned and
> trimmed
> 1½ pounds kosher salt
> 4 ounces (¾ cup packed) brown sugar
> 2 tablespoons cracked black peppercorns
> 6 fresh or dried bay leaves, broken in pieces
> 5 fresh thyme sprigs
> 4 tablespoons juniper berries, crushed
> Food-grade sawdust or wood chips, for smoking

Set the pork belly on a work surface. Find a glass or porcelain dish that holds it snuggly, or cut it crosswise to fit into two containers.

In a large bowl, combine the salt, sugar, and peppercorns and pour about half of the mixture into the curing container. Rub the pork belly generously with some of the remaining mixture and press it into the container. Pack the remaining salt mixture on top so that the pork is completely covered. Cover with wax paper or parchment paper and set on a low shelf in the refrigerator.

Cure the pork for 7 days. Remove it from the container and rinse under cool water to remove any salt that clings to the pork.

Pat the pork dry with a clean tea towel. If the slab is in one piece, cut it in half. Set one piece, fat side down, into a clean dry container. Cover with bay leaves and thyme sprigs, scatter juniper berries on top, and set the second piece of pork, fat side up, on top of the first. Cover with wax paper or parchment and let dry, in the refrigerator, for 1 to 2 days.

Prepare a smoker according to the manufacturer's instructions. Smoke the bacon (see page 144) for at least 8 hours and as long as 36 hours. To test, slice off a piece of bacon and cook it. If it isn't smoky enough, continue to smoke it.

Dry the bacon overnight in front of a slow turning fan, wrap it in parchment paper, and store it in the refrigerator. It will keep for 3 to 4 weeks; you can freeze it for up to 3 months.

To Smoke Bacon

To smoke bacon in a charcoal smoker, begin by soaking food-grade sawdust or wood chips in water. I use an equal mix of cherry, apple, and hickory woods. To begin, light 7 pieces of charcoal (not mesquite) in a chimney starter; transfer the lit coals to the smoker's fire tray. Press the water out of 2 cups of sawdust, and scatter on top of the coals, being careful not to extinguish them. Set the smoking chamber on top of the fire tray, fill the water dish, and set the bacon on the racks. Watch the temperature gauge; it should hover near the low end of the "warm" setting. Smoke should escape through the lid. Check the coals every hour, adding 2 or 3 fresh ones as they burn down. Add more sawdust when the coals are hot.

If you have a portable hot plate or outdoor burner, use dry wood instead of wet. Put a cup or so of chips or sawdust into a wok and heat until it smokes. Immediately pour the smoking chips over the hot coals. Don't do this inside.

Index